Treasures of Darkness

Dear Betty
Keep shining, you
treasure blesses others
as well!

A Prison Journey

TRISH JENKINS

An extraordinary, true story.

Love Trish Jenkins

Author: Trish Jenkins

Title: *Treasures of Darkness*

Subtitle: *A Prison Journey*

Edition: First edition

Publisher: Trish Jenkins (Seasonz Pty. Ltd. Trading as Trish Jenkins)

ISBN: 978-0-646-56039-7

www.speakertrishjenkins.com

DEDICATION

To my Family:

My husband, Justin - A man among men

My parents, Ian and Jan Ross, for giving your all to ensure we got through this as a family.

Dad, thank you for living what you preach.

Mum, you mothered my children for me.

My children, Chelsea, Felicity and Olivia – You are brave little people and true champions.

CONTENTS

ACKNOWLEDGEMENTS

Justin, Chelsea, Felicity and Olivia and the Jenkins family

My parents, Pastors Ian and Jan, and their church, Bribie Island Christian Outreach Centre - You great people stood by your pastors, supporting our family in prayer and writing to me

Wesley Leake and Business Blessings, Ps Clark Taylor and the amazing Campbell family

Friends who wrote, prayed for and encouraged me

Friends, I met later, and who encouraged me to tell my story

The business community who continues to encourage me; you constantly show me that sharing my treasures is worth it

The beautiful women in prison who touched my life

Ps Mark and Leigh Ramsey, and the Citipointe team who continued to support, believe in and encourage me, and support my family

Intercessors who prayed for me

Friends who visited me

Thank you

XX

"And the King will say, 'I tell you the truth, when you did it to one of the least of these my brothers and sisters, you were doing it to me!"

Matthew 25:40

New Living translation

Endorsement

"Trish Jenkins has told her story in a way that will move her readers' hearts and keep them turning the pages! Having undergone a prison journey myself, I recognise the powerful authenticity of this stirring but at times searing account.

Treasures of Darkness also has the encouraging message of how a bruised pilgrim can recover from the depths to a redeemed and rehabilitated life.

I strongly recommend it."

Jonathan Aitken
Former British Cabinet Minister and Member of Parliament
Author, broadcaster, columnist, lecturer and ex-prisoner
Appointed Minister of State for Defence, 1992
Appointed Chief Secretary to the Treasury, 1994
Prisoner for 7 months in 1999
www.jonathan-aitken.com

"I will give you the treasures of darkness and hidden riches of secret places,

That you may know that I, the LORD, Who call you by your name, am the God of Israel."

Isaiah 45:3

New King James Version

GLOSSARY OF AUSTRALIAN TERMS

Aborigine	Noun, Indigenous Australian, usually of dark skin
Aboriginal	Adjective of Aborigine, e.g. Aboriginal painting
Banking	Hiding something in the body
Bloke	Man
Cluey	Smart
Cop flack	To suffer grief or retribution
Cop it sweet	Suffer punishment without complaining
Cuppa	Cup of tea or coffee
Dobber, Dog	Tattle-tale
	Person who tells on others, one who curries favour with officers at the expense of other prisoners
Dobbed in	Reported
Donga	Portable room
D.U.	Discipline Unit
Fit	Set of drug utensils
Forby	Officer
Gear	Stuff, possessions, also a "fit"
Give a serve	Tell someone off, "She gave him a serve!"
Give a toss	Give a thought or care, "Didn't give a toss"
Hoik up	Lift up roughly
Jaffas	A chocolate ball covered in an orange shell
Knickers	Underpants
Kafuffle	A big fuss, something going wrong

Murri	Aboriginal person, usually of S.E. Queensland area Different areas/tribal groups have different names
Newby	New person
Off the rails	Crazy, out of control, unlawful
Orright	All right
Sticky-beak	Nosey
Poshies	Snobs, people who think they are superior
Sneak	Person who robs houses while the occupants are in it
Staunch	Honourable, loyal, won't tell on someone
The Bird	A rude finger gesture
Thongs	Summer footwear
Tickled pink	Very pleased, happy
Twig	Realise something, or notice something going on
2IC	2nd in command

PROLOGUE

It was July, 2009. I lay on my back on the empty prison tennis court gazing up at the sky. It was the only time in S1 where there was not a cage ceiling above my head. I still remember how blue the sky was. Our one hour of exercise time outside was almost up.

The other five women from my unit had already gone back into the block for a cigarette or a cold drink. From a short distance the voices of some Murri (Aboriginal) girls called out to me from their unit windows facing the court, "Hey, Sista-girl! You ok? Whaddayadoin?"

I waved a lazy hand to them and smiled. I felt the blue sky like I felt the breeze, soaking it in. It had been so long. I reached up swirling my hands in figure eights. I knew I looked crazy but I didn't care. There was no wire, no bars between me and the deep blue sky.

I blinkered my eyes with my fingers to block the wire side fences from my peripheral view. That's better. I imagined I was free. It felt like for once I was cheating the system that so thoroughly controlled each area of my life, covering me in greyness.

I was six months into an eight-month sentence. Each day felt like a week, each week like a month. This particular stint in S1 was supposed to be a punishment for an incident that got me kicked out of the minimum security facility known as Helena Jones Community Centre at Albion in the heart of Brisbane. Instead, S1 was a relief. The conditions were Spartan but felt more like a spiritual retreat giving my shattered nerves rest.

The women I shared a unit with were supposed to be the worst, but I found them very easy to get along with. How sad to be in a category where you are considered bad even by prison standards! How much rejection can a person take?

I liked these women better than the catty ones who acted superior. These ones didn't have to prove how tough they

1

were. They didn't get caught up in politics or nasty backstabbing. They called a spade a spade; well actually, they called a spade a #$%&* spade, but I hardly noticed. I just saw precious women being their kind of normal.

They thought I was a bit odd but harmless. I was a "one-eighty-straighty," (both morally and socially). I didn't swear, didn't "swing," was "nice," and one of them "real" Christians; possibly misguided but well-intentioned. They indulged me. I liked them.

Perhaps I was seeing them the way God sees them?

****

If someone had told me in January 2009 that less than two years later I would be on a platform speaking to 500 people about my prison experience I would have blinked in bewilderment.

Yet that public "outing" was just the beginning.

I'd been so ashamed I didn't want anyone to know of my failure.

Imagine the worst thing you've ever done, the thing you are most ashamed of, eternally available for the public with just one click on Google!

Mine is.

The loss of personal freedom and dignity affects people differently. For some, prison is an escape from the perils of a violent home or even homelessness. For others it is where they catch up with friends, who lead an equally lawless lifestyle. For many, it is just plain damaging.

When asked about what being in prison is like, I sometimes wonder which answer to give. I spent eight months incarcerated and had a variety of locations, people and experiences. I was "managed" by people of questionable competence. It was awful and yet there were times of sublime joy each time I had a victory over the evil that pervaded.

It took time and ministry to heal from the emotional and mental hits I took. However, I was determined not to be beaten. There were times I despaired; an insidious voice taunted me, telling me I had ruined my future and was irreparably damaged, my children would have hang-ups, and I had become preaching material for pious ministers to use.

Yet in the back of my mind I always had hope. Sure I would dip into despair, tears and anger. However, what kept me rising again was my faith in God being able to make *all things work together for good*. My experience would not be wasted, unless I gave up.

The decision to go public was not easily made but I was convinced it was the right one. I had my first book to publish and couldn't do it without people finding out.

My pride became less important than my message.

The feedback from *"Dangerous Wealth,"* (a book on financial and romantic fraud signals and bounce back), was very positive but people also wanted to know how I coped with my prison experience.

This isn't a simplistic "how to" self-help book. I actually had to do what was needed to help myself. If that gives you keys for your life, that's even better.

One thing I know. I choose what that experience means for my life. My perspective dictates my success.

You can change the past and free your future - I did!

This book is made up of three things.

1) Letters I wrote home, which my husband Justin then typed out and emailed to our friends, most of whom were from church, but also some beautiful non-church, non-Christian friends. It turns out some of those friends forwarded the emails to other friends who then requested to be on Justin's list. By the time I was released the email updates were going out to over 100 people and beyond.

These letters helped keep me sane. As events unfolded I would consider how I would describe them for my readers. I wasn't there just for me. I was there for them, for you. I was not going to waste the time God had given me there. In spite of persecution from some staff and prisoners, I had a purpose. I made a difference. I couldn't turn my back on the lowliest woman for fear of what others thought.

As it was, one of my letters got me kicked out of the Helena Jones minimum security facility and back to the Big House three months before my discharge!

2) Journal entries of private thoughts and experiences. I couldn't post these as my mail was read by prison officials. It's interesting to compare what I let people know about at the time, with what was going on behind the scenes.

3) Hindsight comments are *italicised*. It was a year before I could look at my letters again. I still find it hard to believe the journey. I look back and see things that happened from a different perspective now. I alternately want to shout a warning; or reach out and hug the naive, yet brave little person I was in prison. Sometimes when you are in a situation, you don't realise how perilous it is.

Revisiting the memories made the nightmares return for a while. I was told I had Post Traumatic Stress Disorder and that there is no cure. I refused to believe it.

This is my prison experience, raw and real. As such you may find it uncomfortable at times. You may find it weird that I would draw on spiritual strength with such conviction. Even some believers may shudder that I shared my faith in such a hostile environment.

To the Christian I say, "If you are facing adversity and can afford to backslide, your adversity is not bad enough."

My situation was too serious to go through without my God.

Don't think this meant I was a perfect Christian in there.

I wasn't like biblical Joseph in ancient Egypt. I wasn't Corrie Ten Boom, ever forgiving the guards in a Nazi prison. I lost my cool occasionally. I did not act very "Christian" at times. I was living among some very nasty, small minded, unsavoury characters... and then there were the prisoners...

There is a misconception that non-violent offenders are kept away from the really bad offenders. It's not true. Apart from those in S10, a secure block referred to as "Protection" (accommodating ex-police officers, child abusers, those with enemies), everyone is lumped together until they are "classified." This can take months, although it isn't supposed to. I lived with murderers, thieves, drug addicts, prostitutes and more. But I often felt the presence of God with me. I was not alone and believed (because I had to) that my journey would result in a greater purpose.

Now I use my story to impart life, purpose and hope into the lives of others.

You matter.

Prison is a horrible experience regardless of whether your prison is made of bricks and razor wire or made of your attitude and life circumstances.

True freedom is a precious thing.

I just ask that you keep an open mind as you journey with me. Perhaps you will gain strength and maybe some faith of your own..?

NOTE: Spelling and language is Australian, except for the word "jail," which is superseding the traditional "gaol."

"Jail" and "prison" are the same in Australia; unlike the U.S., where prison is much more serious than jail.

U.S. readers can refer to the Glossary of Australian Terms on page v, for slang and prison culture words, when necessary.

COURT – January 21-22, 2009

I've watched countless courtroom dramas and even performed jury duty, but nothing prepared me for sitting in the "dock," as a criminal. I thought, 'this must be what Judgment Day will feel like for those who don't know Christ.'

I was dressed in my smart navy pantsuit and cream blouse, *returned to me ruined months later*. My hair was freshly blonded, *another strategic error*, in a shade that just didn't work for me.

Tip: Never, ever get your hair done by an unfamiliar hairdresser before an important event.

An hour earlier, my parents, my lawyer, barrister and I had been sitting in the ground floor coffee shop like respectable people, waiting until it was time to go up. I was sick with nerves so I went to the bathroom to calm myself – and discovered my pants zipper was broken. Great!

In addition, I was sunburned in an embarrassing way. The previous weekend, my husband Justin had whisked our family away to his sister's house at Hervey Bay to enjoy the beach. I had to borrow a swimming costume which was cut differently to mine so a part of my inner cleavage was exposed.

As the extended family frolicked in the water, I (safety mother) was positioned so the children were between me and the sand. This meant the sun beat toward me from the same side for the whole afternoon. The result was just one, not an even two, but one sunburnt, er... bosom.

And it was starting to itch...

I was not exactly filled with self-confidence.

All I needed to top it all off was for a bird to poop on me!

Court is a frightening process, even when you do trust the judgment will be part of God's plan and not man's. I knew I would go to prison. I'd felt it in my prayer time. The previous week I had watched Corrie Ten Boom's *"The Hiding Place,"* a movie about a woman imprisoned for hiding Jews; and *"Roots,"* the slavery mini-series. I felt as though the Lord were saying, "yes, you will go in, but I'll be with you."

My lawyer advised I would likely be given three to four months, six at the worst. The prosecutor was to tell me later that she thought I would go home with a fully suspended sentence because I hadn't actually stolen anything.

I sat trembling and pale in the dock while the prosecution presented its case. I looked at the impassive face of the officer standing next to me. "I am so scared!" I whispered to him. Was I looking for reassurance? He spoke gently and poured me a cup of water. I wondered if the act were an unexpected kindness or perhaps a behaviour management strategy?

I was prepared for the lead prosecutor to be ruthless but in fact she was quite generous and mentioned many good things I had contributed to their case against the trader who had actually stolen everyone's money. She recommended a head sentence of twelve to twenty-four months.

A head sentence is the maximum you could serve. When you plead guilty, you will usually serve one third before the remainder is suspended or you can apply for parole.

I pled guilty because I was.

Suddenly the judge interrupted and scolded the Prosecutor for recommending such a light sentence. He said she should be asking for three to four years!

I felt the blood drain from my face and heard the sharp intake of my mother's breath behind me. "This is not the way I expected things to go." I thought. I had assumed that a judge hands down a sentence somewhere in between the Defence and the Prosecution's recommendations, "I'm in real trouble!"

It wasn't the first time my assumptions had been overly optimistic. I was being carried away by a force I had no control over. It was terrifying.

My penalty would be reduced if I were able to pay money back to the two people whose funds I had used to pay investors, but I had no means to do so.

To put you in the picture:

I had been a successful property investor; however property is often an "asset rich, cash flow poor," investment. I was looking for cash flow investments. I had studied share trading, only to realise I just didn't have the "knack" for it that the seminar "Gurus" did! Then I was introduced to a fellow who claimed to be a consistently good currency trader.

People would lend him money to trade with and he would pay them interest on it. Anything he made above the interest was his. He had become so popular that he needed a contact person to deal with them, so he could be left alone to trade. I became that conduit.

All the due-diligence I knew how to do at the time, confirmed he was everything he claimed to be.

Six months later, our trader took on a partner. Somehow they gained ASIC approval for a registered managed fund. Its returns would be generated by our trader.

As you can imagine, our confidence, and that of many others, was buoyed. We believed we were dealing directly with someone good enough to be the trader for an official managed fund.

We saw the ASIC stamp of approval as an endorsement. Our understanding was faulty.

Our arrangement remained a private loan which he continued to pay interest on faithfully for a year and a half.

Then he stopped paying.

According to the loan agreements, he did have the right to miss a payment as long as he compounded the interest if he had a bad month. He did this for one month, then another. He said it was getting too hard and that future investors would receive a much smaller return.

Panic ran through the investors and I was the contact. On the one hand I had people rushing to give me more money so they could receive the previous higher interest rate. On the other, I had abusive, threatening phone calls and e-mails demanding money back regardless of the terms of their agreement.

I was in over my head. By the third month and two days before he was due to pay, the trader informed me he would not be paying again. He claimed, "If I take the money out of the market now I will not have enough to use to generate the interest."

At this point I had money I was supposed to give to him, but he was supposed to pay me, so I could pay the investors. I felt caught between a rock and a hard place.

Blindly, not seeing an alternative, and with the best of intentions, I asked him if it would help him if, "just this once," we gave some relief to the investors so he could concentrate on trading with the capital he had. He had committed to compounding the earlier non-payments so he was obliged to trade even better than before. I am a rescuer by nature and felt obliged to "fix" a problem that really wasn't mine to fix. I knew it was wrong, but I felt I had no choice.

He wasn't a fool. He agreed. My obligation was to give him the money. If I had physically transferred the money to him, I would not have been charged. Having his permission to do what I did was not considered relevant by the court.

By this time anyone I might have gone to for advice had invested! This conflict of interest isolated me from good counsel. In my fraud prevention book *"Dangerous Wealth,"* I address the issue of "conflicts of interest," when it comes to mentors.

Here is an important lesson. If you want to go into a project with any leader, they must consciously give up their role as pastor or leader/mentor/employer/up-line in your life and refer you to someone else. They cannot be a spiritual or other influence if their money is in any way connected with you or if yours is with them. They will not be able to remain unbiased. Your relationship will be tainted.

The situation was untenable. I lost my perspective. I justified a misuse of funds, at least in my head. I was convinced that the trader would put things right for the next time. I had to believe it.

I was wrong.

A short time later, the Australian Securities and Investments Commission (ASIC) informed me they were investigating our trader for running an unlicensed managed fund, not a scam. I was to be interviewed and I had the right to obtain legal advice.

A corporate lawyer wasn't convinced I had breached the law but advised me to go into voluntary liquidation. He accompanied me to the interview where I explained what had gone on and what I had done to try to "fix" the problem.

"Let me know what I need to do now to put things right and I'll do it." I said rather naively. "If you just let him keep trading he'll be able to draw the money out of the market and give people their money back."

That raised eyebrows and changed the tone of the interview.

At this point I still believed the trader was genuine.

Our auditor in the liquidation was appointed to audit his books too. It was not until well into that audit, that the liquidator informed us that our trader was a fraud. In addition to having had a different last name in the past, he had also defrauded several major financial institutions.

Two days after my interview our bank accounts were frozen without notice. Going into "voluntary" liquidation meant I suddenly had no control over my finances. All my resources were confiscated. My accounts were frozen. There was no option of paying anyone anything because it could be construed as a preferential payment.

My money paid the liquidators their fees as they sold up my assets; Justin's assets were sold to pay lawyers. We went back to work to keep those lawyers paid. So continued our life until July, 2007, when I was served with papers charging me with breaching the Corporations Act. It was the first day of work at my new job!

My great new job was promoting the services of Corporate Investigator, Michael Featherstone of Phoenix Global. He had been speaking at a networking breakfast. I shared my story with him, expressing my dismay at meeting him too late.

I was so passionate about the importance of his services that he hired me! Mick encouraged me to continue working on my fraud warning signals book, but suggested I write it with women in mind. "By the time they call me I can't help them," he said, "It's too late." So I did.

Mick taught me many of the keys that are in *"Dangerous Wealth: What every Successful Woman Needs to Know to Avoid Being Ripped Off!"*

It took three more years of research and development and during that time, I developed strength of purpose. I needed that to be able to deal with the hurting and hurtful people who lashed out at me.

When an investor, who was also a pastor, found out the money was gone, he came to my house to demand I return his investment, that of his family and the flock he had promoted it to.

I didn't have his money and liquidators had frozen my accounts. I was given an allowance and had to account for spending any more than $100 at a time. I would not have been allowed to give money to some investors and not others regardless of the pastor's demands. He outlined who I should pay in his group and in what order. I asked him "what about everyone else?"

"They are not my problem," he replied. He didn't care how it happened but he believed I needed to replace the funds. I felt bullied, caught between "a rock and a hard place." Even if I had been able to comply, it would be an illegal, "preferential payment." The money had been stolen by the trader anyway but that was irrelevant. His "righteous anger" left me traumatised. Justin was furious at the hypocrisy.

We lived through the upheaval and uncertainty for another year and a half until that fateful day in January 2009 where I would receive a penalty. My losses and what I had suffered in the meantime were not considered relevant. In addition to losing our home and other investments, we had personally lost $104,000 to the trader's fraud.

During this period our financial advisor, who was also our accountant, went into liquidation along with $275,000 of our money. We had been doing a joint venture with him for the purchase of a property development. We later learned through his liquidation, that the funds had instead been used as an option payment and the option ran out!

We weren't going to see that money again either, but we would see a large Capital Gains tax bill for "profit" on our liquidated properties! Some had more than doubled in value. Of course that money was absorbed by the liquidators. Oh yes, it also meant we were obliged to pay back the meagre government family allowance we had been receiving for the preceding two years since our "income" had changed.

So there I was in court, being asked why I had not attempted to pay restitution, as it would have a bearing on my penalty. When I could have restored the funds from my own money, I was not allowed to. Then, when I couldn't, since they had been used up by the liquidator, I was being asked why I hadn't!

The judge gave me one more night at home to talk to my family about our options.

My parents considered mortgaging their property, but Justin and I refused their offer. It wasn't their responsibility. I would do the "time."

That afternoon we took our daughters Chelsea aged ten, and twins Felicity and Olivia aged seven, to the park to fly our kites. It's something I find relaxing. It was a difficult last night with my family. Friends were calling to encourage me, yet all I wanted to do was breath in my girls. Explaining to my eldest what might happen was very distressing. In the end, once again, I put my trust in the Lord and hoped for mercy.

Overnight my mother wrote a letter to the judge, pleading for mercy. The next day the judge was handed the letter. Instead of softening him, he voiced his anger at my mother's suggestion that he appeared to lack compassion; her letter was inappropriate.

I heard my family groan and knew they feared it had made the situation worse.

I had to revise my expectations and hoped my sentence would be a year or less.

My barrister stood to sum up. He informed the judge I had no resources left and no hope of raising any. He hoped the judge would take into account that I had not stolen any money, had lost all my assets already and had simply tried to ease a difficult situation.

It didn't have the desired effect.

I was asked to stand for sentencing. I felt naked and humiliated. A spotlight was on me announcing to the world that I was no good.

Then it came: A "head sentence" of two and a half years to be suspended after eight months.

Amazingly I felt relief. I have a self-preservation mechanism that immediately looks for the upside of any situation, especially when the downside is too ugly.

Some people call it "faith," others call it "denial." I'm not sure what it was in that moment. It's why I believed the trader's lies for so long; but it would serve me well in the ensuing months...

As I was led from the dock I turned to my family and said quickly, "It's not so bad, it's less than a year. I'll be OK."

The judge's comments are a matter of public record. By law I am not permitted to publically give an opinion on the actual sentence. I don't have an opinion anymore because I believe God will use anyone to accomplish His purposes, no matter what their prejudice or motives if any. The judge was God's instrument whether he knew it or not; an instrument in the hands of my God. He had the honour of helping extend the Gospel. Many of the women I was privileged to share with would not have listened to me had I not been one of them.

God had a plan for me that involved eight months of incarceration. I had to think this way or I might have become bitter, which would have rendered me useless, my calling unfulfilled.

DOWN TO THE CELLS – **Thursday January 22**

I was led by a strangely handsome officer through a side door and into a hallway. I thought, 'He can't really be my jailer, he is too good-looking and seems kind.' He asked me if I were OK. I knew I had to present calmly, so I just took a few deep breaths and said, "I'm OK, just a bit overwhelmed."

"This is where I have to handcuff you," he said. I could tell he was gauging how difficult I might become. I'd never seen handcuffs up close and now they were put on my own wrists. They felt heavy and possessive; my hands looked frail and tiny.

Another officer with a moustache came to escort me down an elevator. He said, "Don't be afraid, you are going to be searched by two ladies and it's not like in the movies."

Visions of Nicole Kidman in "Bangkok Hilton" being probed for hidden drugs in her nether regions flashed through my mind.

I repeated silently to myself, 'Think of it as a pap smear, pretend it's just a pap smear!!!'

Fortunately, the strip search did not involve touching and the ladies were quite sympathetic. I was allowed to put my top back on before removing my bottoms so I was not completely naked at any one time. I was required to bend forward and shake out my hair, open my mouth and lift my arms. Some women are asked to lift their breasts but there was no need in my case. I was then instructed to turn around to lift each foot and spread my toes, *of all things*!

I wondered how anyone could conceal contraband between their toes but they were actually looking for needle marks! That struck me as funny.

I had remembered to bring my prescription and my mouth guard in its pink container in my pocket. My dentist had it made because I grind my teeth in my sleep when stressed. These were taken from me and recorded, along with two very sad looking ladies' handkerchiefs. The prescription medication would be distributed by an officer at the specified time, but I was not allowed to have the mouth guard. They wouldn't tell me when I might get it back. Perhaps in eight months?

I had removed my wedding and engagement rings before coming to court, because I didn't trust "the system" with their safe-keeping. I had no idea what level of corruption existed, if any, but I wasn't taking any chances with something so personal. Besides, I didn't want them "tainted" by contact with the prison system.

The strip search ladies advised me, "Do your own time. When you go to the cells, you don't have to tell anyone why you are there. Don't ask questions, keep to yourself. Don't give any personal details about where you live, or your family. You don't want them visiting your home when they get out!"

Great! By nature, I'm a gregarious sticky-beak, who will try to rescue the lost and fix the world's problems. This did not sound promising. I resolved to try to be discreet. 'Like Joseph in prison before he became 2IC of Egypt,' I thought...

They asked me if I was afraid of people in prison. Afraid? Who wouldn't be? I was cluey enough to ask for clarity on that one. They answered, "Does anyone have it in for you? Do you want to be segregated in the Protection Unit or go into the General Population?"

"Oh, 'General,' please." I had enough sense to guess that it would be better to join the main group, than be with people who were despised even by the rest of the prison population. These might be child abusers, or partners of paedophiles or those who have made enemies in the criminal world. Or they might be frightened, naïve women, who want extra protection.

I was taken to a holding cell. It had bright orange bars. My shoes had to remain outside the cell. Strangely, that morning after imagining a cold prison cell, I decided to wear socks. I was grateful now. The cell itself was about ten by ten feet. A solid block bench merged with the back wall. There was a metal toilet without a seat which sat behind a half-wall. There was a little sink with a bubbler activated by a button.

No toilet paper. Do I ask for it if needed? Will they give me some, or mock me and make me suffer?

Eventually I had to ask, and they brought it straight away. I wondered if they brought it to comply with a "duty of care" issue, or because badly behaved guests can make a mess of the cell. These were unpleasant imaginings.

Did I mention the camera up on the ceiling?

I waited for what seemed an eternity. It was the first of many waiting times. Lunch arrived, sandwiches and a little box of pineapple juice with a straw. My request for a soothing hot cup of tea was refused. I was not to see one for a week. I hadn't realised how much I depended on my "cuppa."

I was waiting for a prison van to pick me up and escort me a short distance to the Roma Street "Watch-House." I had heard awful things about the infamous watch-house; however I became so bored, that I actually looked forward to the van's arrival.

While I waited in the stark cell, I practised controlling my thoughts so I wouldn't panic. I sang to keep my spirits up. I discovered a radio speaker with a button in the wall, so I pressed it hoping to hear the time or the news. Instead, I listened to tinny music and eventually danced on my own.

Looking back, I think my mind had shut down, refusing to accept the gravity of the situation. I didn't care that a camera was on me. I had to do something that would normally make me happy, so I danced in my socks, and my suit with its broken fly.

An officer announced the arrival of the prison van. They don't like being referred to as guards; I don't know why. Perhaps it sounds more respectable? Handcuffed again but reunited with my shoes, I was led out through security doors. On the way I noticed a clock. It was only 2.45 p.m.

A sliding door opened on the side of the van, and I stepped up into a small metal room with two pairs of seats, facing one another. A camera watched me slyly from on high, behind a dark Perspex triangle.

No seatbelts.

'Is the risk to health and safety from a road accident less than the risk to health and safety from a seatbelt turned into a weapon?' I would ponder many such incongruities as the "System" unfolded before me.

As the door slammed shut, I flashed back to an amusement park ride, where the attendant slams the protective bar down so you don't fall out. With the handcuffs affecting my balance, I bounced around, jerking forward, back, and sideways, at the whim of the traffic.

I pretended I was on such a ride, until the exhaust fumes crept in and made me feel nauseous.

I remembered reading about the Nazi's; killing Jews by turning the exhaust pipes back into trucks filled with people, driving until they choked to death. Not a comforting picture.

Through the small barred window, I watched familiar landmarks pass by. It was a short trip from the George Street Courthouse to the Roma Street Watch-House. The van wheeled down a driveway and pulled up. A large roller door descended in front while another trapped us behind.

Cave like.

ROMA STREET WATCH-HOUSE

Thurs 22nd – Tues 27th Five nights and six days

Stepping down from my metal box, I was directed through a glass door which was in fact, one side of a transparent cell. Through the other side I could see the processing desk, police, and watch-house staff milling around or tapping at computers.

I had arrived at the Brisbane Roma Street Watch-House - and this time my expectations were not far wrong.

A well-dressed young woman of about twenty-seven sat delicately in the cell. She wore a black suit with a purple blouse; her hair neatly pulled back. She would have passed for a lawyer, were it not for her bare feet! My shoes had been removed again, too.

This beautiful, sad young woman would become a close friend and ally for the next few months. She smiled tremulously, "What are you in for?" Hmm, so much for keeping to myself. We told each other our respective stories.

Amanda had been in five years earlier for having a car accident, in which someone was badly hurt. She had been over the legal alcohol limit. Consequently her driver's licence was suspended for ten years. This was her seventh year without a licence and without a drink. One slip and here she was again.

Amanda was able to let me know what to expect. "This is the worst it will ever get. It's Thursday, so hopefully we'll be taken out to the proper prison at Wacol, before the weekend."

"Is that because there is nothing to do here?" I asked.

"No, it's because we don't want to be here when they bring in the weekend 'riff-raff.'"

From time to time, we watched bedraggled individuals being processed and fingerprinted. Then they disappeared deeper into the intestines of the mysterious building.

As we got to know one another I was moved by Amanda's plight. She was mortified that she had blown it, and wept. I got the attention of a police officer, who appeared to be part of a group of officers standing around waiting for someone or something, and asked politely for a tissue. He looked at Amanda with an expression of annoyance and said, "Use your sleeve!" He turned away to resume his chat.

Our status at the bottom of the pile was established.

It was Thursday 22nd January 2009. We ended up staying for a long weekend because Monday 26th was the Australia Day public holiday. My companion was right about the "Weekend riff-raff!"

Did you know you are only one bad car accident away from prison yourself?

We want to control our lives, but it's as futile as spitting in the wind. You can have as much asset protection as you like, but your kingdom is still only a house of cards. Any day, any moment, it can be taken from you.

Mine was... but I eventually discovered greater riches.

Would you?

Or would you wallow in self-pity? If you are a Christian, would you backslide (turn away from God) in anger because things did not go the way you believed they should have?

Just a thought.

On many occasions leading up to court, the Lord had made it clear that everything would turn out all right. In the back of my mind I knew that His idea of "all right" and mine could be very different! I had to trust Him to bring me through whatever was coming.

I did not believe I was being punished by God. I still don't. I was being retrained, given a new experience, so that when I spoke into people's lives again, it would be of things that really matter.

...BACK TO THE WATCH-HOUSE

Eventually it was my turn to be processed. To the side of the general processing area were piles of men's clothing: work shorts, T-shirts, track suit pants and tops, the kind without zippers. These were referred to as "Browns" because of their colour.

After selecting the smallest sizes I could find, I was taken behind a curtain by a female officer. Once again I was strip searched, but this time I had to squat. It's common for women to carry drugs in their bodies.

To lighten the moment and minimise my embarrassment, I warned the officer that if anything did come out, it was because I had given birth to twins, and my pelvic floor muscles weren't what they used to be.

She didn't laugh either...

"If you are wearing a tampon you need to pull it out and show me. You'll be given some padded plastic underwear instead." Eek! Fortunately that wasn't an issue for me that week, and I breathed a silent prayer of thanks.

My own clothes, including bra and "undies" were taken away. I now wore gappy, men's work shorts for underwear. Great! At least they were soft, presumably from their many wears and washes.

Dressed in our "browns," Amanda and I were issued a thinly woven "waffle" blanket, and a threadbare towel.

It was time to go deeper into our dungeon.

We were led past computers where the normal looking people tapped and moved papers around. We passed "padded" cells that looked frightening and the padding didn't look soft, more like canvas. On we went through security doors and down corridors, through more security doors and another corridor. At least that's what it felt like. I lost my bearings.

21

We passed glass rooms where tattooed men in "browns" stood to stare at us. We looked straight ahead, walking until we were ushered into a glass room of our own.

The room was rectangular. Its interior wall had two glass doors opening into smaller rooms at the rear. The front room contained a TV high on the wall, and a metal picnic table with bench seats bolted to the floor. It was a common room that prisoners would share for a few hours a day. To the side was a large metal door I would later learn contained a shower. It was locked. A painted line ran across the inside of the entrance. We were not to cross the painted line. The doorway was to be kept clear at all times.

The rooms made up a "pod." Our "pod" consisted of the "common room" and the two glass cells at the rear for sleeping. Some pods were longer and had more cells. Ours was painted a sickly, depressing, institutional green, some others were painted blue.

There were no beds as such. Rather, from each side wall emerged a low platform that would fit a body stretched out. On each platform (and propped against its wall) were three square vinyl seat cushions. These would serve as our mattresses.

At the end of one platform, a low wall came out, and then sloped diagonally down before dropping to the floor. It shielded the toilet but allowed anyone outside to see the user's head and shoulders, probably their feet too if they had long legs.

The metal commode had no seat; however it did have a little sink with a tap and drinking bubbler built into the cistern at the top.

The whole pod was filthy. It stank of men's urine; the pungent smell telling tales of unhealthy, unclean living. The floor was covered in grit and dirt that gathered in the corners. We were barefooted, of course.

A feeling of darkness crept over me. I considered the various kinds of evil that had stayed here. What demons had taken up residence in this place of misery? Would I be up to the spiritual warfare required?

This was where the "rubber met the road." I had to live my faith.

I thought back to the "Training in the Spirit" our church had been known for in earlier days. How I wished at that moment that I had pursued those things instead of getting caught up in wealth creation.

Still, I reminded myself of the Corrie Ten Boom story. Corrie had been arrested for helping Jews in Holland during WWII. She was frightened but then her father asked her, "When you go to the station, when are you given your ticket?"

"When we need to use it," she answered.

"So too with God, He gives us the courage we need when we need it and not before."

I breathed a prayer to the Lord trusting Him to give me courage in that frightful place. The scary part is not when things are moving along; it is when you are settled and have time to think about your surroundings. Turning around, I saw very rough looking men staring at us from a few feet away, No bars, just transparent, reinforced glass separated us. Some of those men would be there for minor offences, but there were also likely to be rapists, child molesters, the violent and murderers among them.

There was also a large pod full of men dressed in white hospital gowns. We quickly deduced they were not even permitted to wear the shorts for underwear. These were the mentally defective criminals. What kind of women would join us over the next little while?

I would soon find out.

I was allowed one phone call. I let my family know where I was, and that I was alright. None of us had been able to find out earlier what the procedure would be. Even my own barrister had wrongly said that I would go to the Arthur Gorrie Remand Centre, but I quickly learned "Arthur Gorrie" is a men's only prison! His ignorance annoyed me. I wondered what else he was ignorant about that might have helped me. His scope of service stopped at the court room and strictly within the allotted billable hours.

I'll never know if I would have been better off with Legal Aid. Justin was not legally obliged to finance my lawyer, but he fought as hard as he could to get me the best advice. Perhaps we should have paid less, and trusted God more. Ah well, "coulda, shoulda, woulda...didn't!"

That single, five minute phone call was extremely difficult. I had practical matters for Justin to deal with. I briefly spoke to my traumatised parents; unfairly insisting they do not fall apart in front of our daughters.

Finally, I spoke with my dear little girls who'd had their first day at a new school and didn't understand why I wasn't at home to hear all about it. I struggled to keep the tears from my voice.

Only the grace of God sustained us.

In the pod, Amanda and I decided to make the best of things. That meant scrubbing down the cell. We had no equipment, so we wet the cheap, thin, squares of toilet paper with water from the bubbler. It was fortunate that we found dregs of soap to rub against our makeshift cleaning rags.

We soaped all over the basin and toilet cistern, the bowl, the floor, the protrusions of wall we were to sleep on; and wiped over the vinyl cushions. There was nothing else to do so we wiped down the walls and glass panels as well. We would not be able to clean the shower until the next day when we were allowed to use it. When we did we would find it filthy with hair, soap scum and other unidentified, but no doubt, unhygienic specimens. It irked us that we had no footwear.

Using the commode was a challenge. It had no seat and not enough privacy to "hover." We agreed that our scrubbing had to be thorough enough to allow us to sit. The other person would stand in a place that blocked the view of the men, as much as possible. There was one Asian man in particular, who each time climbed up on his pod's table, craning his neck to get a look at us peeing. It was truly creepy.

On the second day, I noticed the back of my thighs felt bruised. I realised it was from the narrow curved metal of the seat-less toilet. Yeah, "great" again. Sunburnt, itchy, peeling boob, bruised thighs, and men's loose shorts for underwear. Welcome to your next calling, Trish!

Late in the afternoon, we were locked in our inner cell so that dinner could be passed through a little slot within the door. Plastic knives and forks accompanied an "airline" type meal with a pineapple juice box.

Dire circumstances create an intimate atmosphere. We were both glad not to be alone. This stranger became a valued friend as we shared our fears and experiences. I had the privilege of introducing her to Christ. We used a scrap of bread from dinner and the juice for communion. I was able to minister inner healing to the hurts in that lovely young woman's life. She was the first of many I was privileged to pray for in the coming months.

Sleep was elusive. I was used to two pillows and the comfort of my husband's arms. Instead we each lay on the firm, brown, vinyl cushions with just the thin waffle blanket. I used my track suit top and towel as a makeshift pillow. I prayed for sleep, and that I would not wake up with a crick in my neck, or a headache.

Sleep was broken by torches regularly shining on us, and the noises of unruly men.

In the morning we had the unexpected surprise of a cooked breakfast. We concluded the caterers also had the contract for an airline as we examined the spoonful of strange looking scrambled egg, toast, tomato, mini-sausage, and pineapple juice. We thanked our host politely as we passed our containers and cutlery through the small opening in the door again. We were both from "respectable" homes after all.

Lunch was usually a salad roll and pineapple juice. Dinner was a cold airline packet with the ever faithful pineapple juice. The meals were tiny and didn't fill me even with my small build. I wondered how some of these large men coped with so little to sustain them. I thought it was just as well they had no calorie burning activities to do. We wondered if the minimal food was a behaviour management strategy. Less food = less energy = less trouble.

I ate everything and still lost over five kilograms (about eleven pounds) during my stay.

In the morning we were allowed into the common area of the pod, no one was yet in the other inner cell. We were each issued a disposable plastic cup with a tiny toothbrush in it, which had to be screwed together. The teeth, of hard plastic, were very short (about a quarter inch), and sat in just two short rows. A scrap of toothpaste had already been applied for us. Also in the cup was a tiny soap sealed in paper, like those you find in a motel.

We waited. Eventually, we heard a buzz and the heavy, metal door that hid the shower cubicle opened. Our good manners were at odds with our surroundings:

"Would you like to go first?"

"Oh no, you go ahead. I'll wait."

"Are you sure? Thanks so much, you go first, next time."

The power in each kind word was magnified in that unpleasant place. I very quickly saw that as a key to self-preservation. "Do not be overcome by evil, but overcome evil with good." (Romans 12:28).

When it was my turn, I contemplated the little room. Metal walls with a filthy little metal shelf moulded in the corner,

26

presumably for my towel and clothes; and some little bumps in the metal floor to prevent slipping. No taps, just a shower rose and a button. I pressed it expecting cold water to spray me or a tiny trickle to dribble down the wall. I was surprised to have a proper shower, until it stopped automatically after three minutes. I dried off and dressed in the same shorts and T-shirt that served as underwear and pressed the button to be let out again.

Ill-fitting replacements weren't issued until Sunday. It was the only change of clothes we were given in the six days we were there.

A small rectangle of polished metal was screwed to the wall above our basin to serve as a mirror. It was so high we had to stretch to see a cloudy image of our faces. I don't remember if we were issued a comb. We had nothing for our skin.

Six days without moisturiser in air-conditioning takes its toll. By the time I got to the prison my face was tight and my lips were so badly chapped that pieces of hard, broken skin were standing up like razors. Both sides of my mouth were split.

It was Friday, and a new member was introduced to our pod.

Bernice was a large, foul mouthed young woman with long, thick hair, very pale skin and rotten teeth. She sailed in, announced she was having withdrawals from heroin, went straight to the other cell and lay down to sleep. My first close contact with what was obviously a "hardened" criminal!

Amanda and I looked at each other and wondered what we were in for when she awoke. The reading I had done regarding withdrawals painted a frightening picture of screaming pain, vomiting, diarrhea, and flinging oneself about for several days.

Our next guest arrived and we pointed to the cell where Bernice was sleeping.

She looked frightened, and asked us anxiously, "Will she attack me?" Not having a clue, we answered, "No, you'll be safe, she's

OK." We did our best to reassure her but we weren't the ones sharing a cell with Bernice!

Francis was a young woman with big curls, a baby face and sad eyes. She had worked in the payroll office of a supermarket. She was also a gambling addict. Her job provided her the opportunity to misdirect funds she could then use to gamble with. She is still amazed at how easy it was to create fictional employees.

Francis came from a blended, yet respectable home. She didn't drink much or do drugs. However, she had begun buying scratch-it cards as a lonely young teenager, quickly becoming addicted. She was to serve fourteen months.

In the afternoon, an uproar of catcalls arose from down the corridor. As we craned our necks, we watched in awe as a young wild-haired Indigenous woman strode towards us. With blanket and towel in one hand, the other flipped "the bird" to the male prisoners as she swept past them.

Sophie entered our pod like it was her lounge room, dumping her gear, flopping down with a big grin and a string of profanity.

We liked her instantly.

There was something reassuring about her confidence. I was fascinated. She had got caught with drugs at Southbank, a popular city play area where families gather and security is greater. Cops can generally tell when someone is suspect, and she and her boyfriend just looked, well, suspicious. Giving cheek is a quick way to get more attention from the police, too, even if you are not doing anything wrong.

Sophie was familiar with a variety of watch-houses. She claimed to have miscarried in one due to a police beating. I didn't know if she was telling the truth, but from what I have heard and observed since, it wouldn't surprise me. There are many stories from Indigenous women about police brutality but they are difficult to prove.

I remembered the "Aboriginal Deaths in Custody Inquiry," being big news in the late 1980's and early '90's. Aborigines were committing suicide in alarming numbers, whilst in custody. It was even higher in remote areas. I thought then, of the questions raised by the media, about whether they had indeed been "suicides." I hadn't really believed the accusations back then. After all, the police are there to "serve and protect." However, now I can see how easily a "line" gets crossed. A criminal lacks credibility, and can be severely punished for making an accusation that cannot be proven. Why would they be believed?

Some of the officers we encountered were polite and matter-of-fact. Others were profane, verbally abusive and rude. As far as some were concerned, we were the dregs of society. I wondered at the irony of filthy language being against the law, and yet used with impunity by some officers.

Police and corrections officers have difficult, often unpleasant, jobs. I'm sure most of them are well-intentioned, "good" people. However, personalities and strength of character vary under pressure; so it's little wonder some of them become tainted by their environment.

People like me are not normally bothered by police. As a well-mannered, well-dressed, white woman, I have "respectable" written all over me. By comparison with many women, I have *nothing* to complain about. In prison I made a point of being polite to everyone, especially officers, regardless of how they spoke to me. I carefully worded my requests, so they would respond favourably. I didn't feel like a criminal, I didn't see myself as a criminal, so I didn't talk to them like I was inferior. This didn't always endear me to some staff, but those stories will come later.

The next morning, Bernice awoke, crying out in pain. She was very sick. She had run out of useable veins, so she'd given herself an extra dose into her upper arm muscles. Apparently it would be less powerful, but it lasted longer. *Later on someone else told me that theory was rubbish.*

We let Bernice have the first shower of the day. She didn't bother closing the heavy door. She had trouble lifting her badly swollen arms, so I helped her remove her top (sticky from dried pus), and winced when she exploded a string of invectives from the pain. She was like a big wounded animal.

Bernice had been here before. As we waited for our turn we heard the water stop... then start again. We looked at each other, realising we could have had a longer shower just by pressing the button again! Bernice wordlessly took three showers. We weren't going to complain! Eventually she emerged, moaning in pain. She tried to dry off, but needed help.

I noticed a hole in each of her upper arms, one centimetre, or almost a half-inch, in both diameter and depth. The skin around the holes was red, tight and swollen. I looked inside and could see her muscle sitting deeper within. I'd never seen a wound like it. Both holes were dribbling a thick yellow substance, watery in parts, as it oozed like poisonous toothpaste from the expanded punctures. It descended down each arm rapidly, and stained her shirtsleeves.

She told me it was heroin. I sprang for the cheap and nasty toilet paper, the kind you find frustrating in public toilets. I must have gone through half a box wiping gently up her arms.

The other girls whispered in horror, "Don't touch her, you don't know what she's got!"

I knew they were referring to HIV. I ignored them and continued wiping the tender arms, quietly ministering to Bernice, silently praying for her. She had a need and I could help. I firmly believed that regardless of what she "had," God would not let me catch anything if I was serving Him by serving her.

My actions were naïve, perhaps even noble; but still, it gave me a charge, as I felt the power of the Holy Spirit's anointing, moving from me to Bernice. She felt it too and, looking in my eyes, she asked, "What the #$%&* was that?"

A peculiar friendship was born.

I didn't have any cuts on my hands, and I was sensible enough to wash thoroughly with soap afterwards. Fortunately, Bernice was taken to see a nurse who put band-aids on her holes.

Our time at the watch-house was mind-numbingly boring. A highlight was when we were randomly moved to other pods. It happened several times. Then we would scrub all over again. An officer told us it wasn't our job. He said he'd get us a broom but we didn't see one. We asked if a cleaner came in, and were told, "Oh yes, every couple of days." We never saw one of those either. He was probably being sarcastic!

Another highlight was being allowed to spend an hour in the yard each day. This was a brick pit, a small outdoor area made of high brick walls and the sky. It had a putrid toilet at the rear, with a bubbler in the top that we were not going to risk drinking from. There was nothing to do in it but walk up and down.

I thought of the many times I had walked into the city from Roma Street Station, totally unaware of the misery just a few metres below me.

Making the most of the novelty of fresh air and sky, I pulled off my tracksuit top, tied it into a ball and tossed it to Amanda, "Catch!" She laughed, and we all began to toss it around, pretending to score goals. This game was popular each time we went out. Then one day the voice of a rather unpleasant officer yelled at us, telling us "not to play" with the piece of uniform, or we'd be "put inside" again.

We amused ourselves by doing hand stands against the walls for a while. It may sound silly, but there was nothing to do but stand around. I thought it was important to create a positive atmosphere for us. I'm not sure where I was mentally, but I felt spiritually responsible for these women. That meant making the best of things.

Another game I suggested was the "silly walk" game. This game had one main rule. Each person had to move across the yard in a different way. I'm sure the officers wondered what they were dealing with, as we skipped, waddled and danced back and forth! I had these girls laughing, which was so much better than crying.

"Well, that was a pleasant hour." I commented one day as we made our way inside; as though we had been ladies strolling in a garden!

Bernice cackled. "Pleasant, eh? Oh this was soooo *pleasant*! You called this @#&* hole *'rather unpleasant'* today. Who talks like that? You are so funny! I'm calling you 'Pleasant' from now on!"

So, she did. I had a soft spot for Bernice. She didn't accept Christ, but she accepted me.

I laughed at myself and took it as a compliment. I knew I was an "odd duck" in this place. I felt like a visitor passing through. It was strange, like being caught in an episode of the Twilight Zone.

Bernice referred to the officers as "Forbys," pronounced "Fourbies." It's rhyming slang for screw: 4B2 (4x2 plank) - screw! We are not allowed to call them "Screws." There is some dispute over the origin of referring to prison officers as "Screws."

It could refer to "thumbscrews" as an instrument of torture, or a box with a crank that prisoners were required to turn so many times a day. A warden could make the turning easy, or hard, by the turning of a screw. It could also refer to a screw being used to lock prisoners' cells, instead of a key.

I was in prison without having stolen anything. For a while I would feel obliged to explain this as I met people, officers in particular. It was as though I were clinging to innocence. I felt a need for people to know I didn't really belong there. It was faulty thinking.

I saw a distinction between those who should be there, and those who shouldn't. While I still think there are people there who shouldn't be there, my faulty thinking was that I was somehow a better kind of sinner than the rest.

Eventually, I would acknowledge and repent of that pride. I was no better than these women; regardless of the crimes committed. In God's eyes, we are all the same. None of us is "innocent." We either have a relationship with Him, or we don't, and that is based on our acceptance of Christ paying for our sin, not because we are nice, or clever, or rich, or anything.

Pecking orders occur everywhere and God hates them. I am different, because of my education and training, my family, my faith, my mental, spiritual and emotional development. That doesn't make me superior. I have *skills* that are of *value*, but it certainly doesn't make *me* of more *value* than any other human being. I do talk differently from most people who go to prison; I don't swear, and I have hope.

However, that was not always going to be an advantage to me.

In fact, at times it would make me a target.

I was determined not to succumb to the "attitudes" of negativity and despair that plague the prison population.

I didn't always succeed.

The watch-house remains in my memory as a peculiar time. It could be particularly nasty, as a deterrent, to those who are hauled in for a few hours or overnight, after being a public nuisance. Perhaps it is thought that a few hours in Hell might make them mend their ways. Or, more likely, men are there for such a short time that it doesn't matter. I'd been informed my stay would be three days at the most. It was six with only one change of clothes in that time.

Men are delivered to their prison almost daily due to the turnover. We got to chat to a few through the glass. Some were there for fighting. Some were hauled in drunk and disorderly. Others faced more serious charges. The mentally ill men were disturbing. They are the criminally unbalanced. Sometimes they are schizophrenic and/or bi-polar. If not taking the right medication, they can get into real strife. There were also those who might try to hurt themselves. We had walked past empty "padded" cells. I heard ugly stories about what could go on in those.

I met a young woman who claimed to be a firebug. Her eyes held a strange expression as she described her fascination. I'm sure demons of mental illness stared back at me.

"Duty of care" is a difficult thing in a place where people are so damaged. I was to observe the "box-ticking" attitude towards "care," during my sentence, and it was frightening.

One of the girls we met was particularly cheeky and flirtatious. She stirred up the men so much, the officers threatened the men with cell lockdown (no access to the common area where the TV was), if they spoke to us. It didn't stop the mental ones from trying to attract our attention, making lewd requests, or lifting their "hospital gown" to show us their "privates." I did my best to ignore them.

During the many hours of inactivity, I sang to the girls, prayed, and read out loud from a little Gideon's Bible Amanda had been given. Because of her alcoholism, she was allowed an AA (Alcoholics Anonymous), book and the bible. Bernice had never heard any Bible stories before, and was puzzled by the strange man Jesus, with his odd advice on life.

One officer gave us some out-of-date magazines from the staff room. The next day, another officer yelled abuse and accused us of stealing them. How ridiculous! If any of us had been able to sneak out for anything, it wouldn't have been to return with magazines!

No smoking is permitted in the watch-house. Several women vowed to use the opportunity to give up, for good. I felt sorry for the smokers. I could relate to them, because I was not permitted to have a cup of tea. I love my tea. A nice hot "cuppa" cures many ills.

Tuesday 27th January

Eventually, the time came for Amanda and me to be escorted back through the maze to the van secreted between the roller doors. It reminded me of the larger horse-floating trucks you see on the road, the kind that have doors in the sides and little windows high up; only these doors were too narrow for a horse.

Now when I see a prison truck, out and about, I wonder about the wretches inside and what misery they face. The other girls were not included in our trip to Brisbane Women's Correctional Centre (BWCC) at Wacol, a western suburb on the outskirts of Brisbane; instead, we shared the truck with some men. Handcuffed again, we climbed up through a side door into the metal cavity. The men were on the other side, separated by a metal wall, but we could see through a crack in the panels to talk a little bit.

It disturbed us that they knew our surnames, and wanted to stay in touch. They had been able to see the list of prisoners' names on the board; behind where the officers had sat in their "fishbowl." That was creepy.

It was a long trip out to Wacol. We felt quite sick from the exhaust fumes that crept into the cavity where we sat. We entered the men's prison first, between gates topped with razor wire, then pulled up inside a secure shed. An officer escorted the men through a door. We were allowed out, because the truck's air-conditioning didn't work with the motor off, and it was Summer-time.

Our trip resumed. BWCC wasn't much further. It struck me as ironic that a prison was surrounded by beautiful countryside with kangaroos grazing near the menacing layers of razor wire fencing.

We pulled up in a shed similar to the earlier one. From there we were ushered through a security door that oddly reminded me of the staff entrance at the rear of a shopping centre. I'd often used such doors in my sales career. Perhaps my mind was trying to normalise my surroundings to preserve my sanity, and minimise my apprehension.

We entered a reception area where we waited once again. It could have been any office in any business except for the outfits. Women in officer's uniforms tapped on computers. Women in blue polo shirts and grey shorts cheerfully moved about. They welcomed us and helped find similar outfits for us. We were issued with uniforms and bedding in a white feed sack, the kind you see filled with grain at a farm supply store. We were handed a brown paper bag containing a "black and gold," (generic) label toothbrush, toothpaste, deodorant, soap and a plastic comb. It also contained a set of scuffed plastic picnic crockery and cutlery.

We were able to have a cold shower before exchanging our watch-house "browns," for the blue prison uniform. Each of us was photographed. There were questions asked and forms filled out. The officer processing me came to a section called "Distinguishable Markings."

"What tattoos do you have?"

"No tattoos." I answered.

"Well, keep it that way; getting any while you are here is an offence." I had no intention of getting a tattoo as a souvenir of prison, but it wasn't long before I met people who accumulated them.

One of the things that struck me as very odd was the number of female officers who looked like men. Their hairstyles and posture were masculine and their body shapes were large or solid. I naively thought they carried themselves that way, because they must appear strong to the inmates.

It wasn't until later that I realised, up to half of the officers were "butch" lesbians. Many of the inmates were, too. It's one stereo-type that proved to be true. I have lesbian friends and I don't expect non-Christians to behave with Christian morals, be they gay or straight. However, it was unsettling to wonder why so many of them work in a women's prison. (It's also unsettling to be strip searched by them). Was there a deliberate agenda; or were they part of a secret "club" that did favours for one another, like with Freemasonry? I didn't want to think about the spiritual strongholds behind that idea.

It occurred to me that the officers were just as much prisoners as me. I would leave one day but they were stuck here.

Part of the processing was a quiz from the nurse. Apart from the usual general health questions, there was interest in whether I had ever been abused, molested, raped, addicted to drugs or other substance, or treated for psychological disorders. "No," I answered, to all.

I asked the nurse what percentage of women coming through had been sexually abused.

"Ninety-six percent," she answered. I was surprised. I already knew that abused children often go "off the rails," and end up in prison or creating dysfunctional homes of their own. It occurred to me that had there been no abuse, women's prisons might be virtually empty. Often a woman's life is taken off course by abuse. Abuse creates despair, depression and self-loathing; emotional pain is alleviated by promiscuity and drug use.

Eventually crimes are committed to pay for drug use. Sometimes a woman is born into a family already in that cycle. Sometimes they are romantically linked to a criminal and are trapped in that culture.

Many women are prisoners of their life choices without ever having gone to prison.

Others are set free from the cycle; however, that doesn't happen without help. I have a new respect for ministries like "Drug Arm" and "Teen Challenge." I'd like to catch our young women before they make life changing choices, based on anger and rebellion. Our youth are of such infinite value, yet are only a *few choices* away from greatness or destruction. Many feel powerless. I'd like to remind them of the power of choice.

My urine test was clean of course. "You are hungry," she said.

"How did you know?" I asked.

Your ketones are up; see?" She showed me the analysis chart.

The nurse gave me a clean sample jar with lanolin in it for my damaged lips. I wanted to cover my whole face with it.

I was assigned an identification number. I had to memorise that number, as it would be used for my telephone code, my access to other areas of the prison, and my order forms. While I was at the watch-house, Justin had driven out to the prison to submit visitor applications, and place some money in a trust account for me to use. This account paid for the toiletries I was given in the brown paper bag. I was allowed to place an order for stationery, a limited variety of sweets, and personal items.

Finally, we each clipped a plastic photo ID with our number on it, to our collar, which permitted us to move between secure buildings, when necessary.

It was time to see our new home.

BWCC - BRISBANE WOMENS CORRECTIONAL CENTRE, WACOL

S7 (Secure Block 7)

Induction Unit

During the first few days in S7, I wrote as much as I could remember about court, the Watch-House, and my first impressions. There wasn't much else to do, and I wanted to capture the extraordinary experiences. They make up many of the preceding pages.

Eventually, we were led, dragging our sacks, to S7, the Induction Unit. This is where we would be observed for a few days, before being fed into other units. It's also where we were informed of the rules. Each unit was like a large hall with cell doors lining three walls on two levels, with a wide staircase leading up to the second level. The second level just had a walkway going around, enabling access to the cells. We were not allowed on the stairs during the day.

In the afternoons, we could choose to be locked in our cells for two hours, or stay downstairs in the hall for that time. One end of the hall had tables with seats fixed to the floor. Nearby, two mesh picnic benches allowed women to sit, uncomfortably, and gaze up at a TV that rarely worked. At the rear, a Coke machine got over-worked, and a single exercise bike sometimes got worked. The fourth wall contained the entrance and the "Fishbowl," an office area with a barred window, from which officers could supervise both us and the unit on the other side, through another barred window.

To one side of the unit were some windows and a door, opening to a concrete yard about the size of a large lounge room. It was caged with what appeared to be the square mesh used to reinforce concrete. A basketball hoop hung at the far end. A telephone was fastened to a side wall. Once our ID number was connected to the phone system, we could make ten minute phone calls before being cut off. Two long benches were provided for women to sit on, while endlessly queuing for their turn on the phone. There was often a conflict, when the noise of the basket-ball hitting the backboard made listening on the phone difficult.

A great variety of people pass through S7, from respectable pensioners caught for earning undeclared income, to serious drug and/or violent offenders. The only people we did not encounter were those in "Protection." This was a special unit, commonly referred to by my fellow prisoners as "The Boneyard." These women were spoken of with scorn and malice.

At any one time, around 3% of Queensland women are in prison. According to a government commissioned Women in Prison report, recidivism (repeat offending) dropped from 34% to 25% where education programs were participated in. If we average those figures we can roughly say that 2% of Queensland women (66% of ex-prisoners) do not re-offend. With the exception of murderers, most sentences served seem to be less than two years. So, if 2% of the female population is always in prison, and prisons have a turn-over of different women every two years or less, that means a very large proportion of the population has done time. (I'd like a mathematician to work that one out.)

What that means is that you have no idea if your neighbour, your boss, or your friend, has a record. They won't tell you. There is no "Mark of Cain" on their heads. What I can tell you is that they cannot leave this place without being damaged.

The person you judge as a "no-hoper," may very well be so damaged, that they really don't have any hope left.

The little bit of education they receive in prison, is supposed to help women become more employable. However, that is becoming increasingly difficult as more companies require a criminal history check to help screen job applicants.

The irony is that some of these women would make better, more honest, employees than anyone else. Why? Firstly, they would not do anything to risk going back to prison. Secondly, they know they would be the first people suspected of anything. Thirdly, they are of the small percentage that was actually caught. If you're in business, your own staff could be among the latter.

Fewer women break the law than men. Consequently, more resources are directed to men's prisons. Even something as simple as our sun hats were oversized, because they were originally from the men's prison.

BWCC is overcrowded, so it is common to have two women share a cell, designed for one occupant. Amanda and I were glad to bunk in together. One of us would have to wedge her mattress between the bed and desk. The desk was shallow and fixed to the wall. A little TV sat on it. At the end of the desk were some open shelves, and under the desk, a metal seat could swing out; but not when the mattress was on the floor. It was a very economical use of space.

Beyond the shelves was the toilet over which a mirror was fixed. Opposite the toilet was the shower corner. The shower space was shielded by a wall that separated it from the bed frame in front. A barred window in the rear wall gave a forlorn view. On the ceiling, of the "bathroom" end, a domed or "convex," mirror enabled an officer (male or female), to see you behind the shower wall. They checked on us every two hours through a small rectangular window in the heavy cell door.

The best way to describe how it feels to live like this is to suggest you pick up a crackly, vinyl-covered pillow, a blanket and an unreliable, little TV set, then go and live in your bathroom for eighteen hours a day with a stranger!

Oh, and have an even stranger male, or butch lesbian, stare in at you, every two hours, shining a torch in your face. Hopefully, you won't be taking care of personal matters when they do.

The following diagram is not in exact proportions but it will give you an idea:

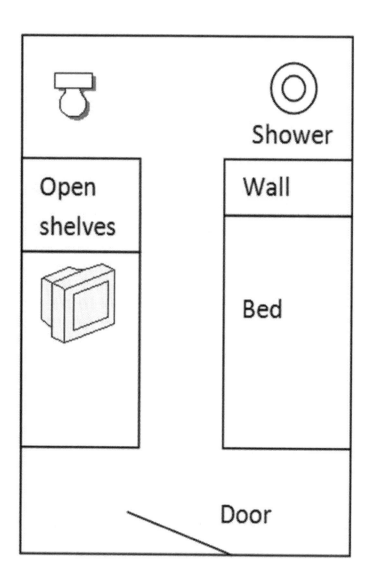

I got to know a number of the women, and was relieved to see a chaplain wander through. Being able to connect with a chaplain was very encouraging. They were people from my culture, regardless of the denomination. I had seen one, briefly, at the watch-house; but was not permitted to talk to her for more than a few seconds. No services were held in "Hell."

When some of the women learned I was a Christian, they came to me with prayer requests. I was moved by their simple faith. I expected hostility, and would find it, "down the track"; but not from this group. I was just as interested in these women as they were with me.

I had never seen track marks from heroin up close before, now I had plenty of opportunities to examine them! Several ladies were only too happy to educate me about such things.

I looked for encouragement wherever I could find it. One night Amanda and I watched *"The Bucket List"* movie on our little TV. We decided to make our own bucket lists for when we got out. We were going to appreciate our freedom and live life to the full.

It's probably a good thing I didn't know that having a criminal conviction would cut my list in half. Or at least put off my ability to do them for a number of years.

It was here I began writing notes about my journey.

Journal notes

Friday 30th January, 2009.

God's grace is sustaining me. I am amazed that I still haven't cried. I don't feel the need to yet. I'm sure I will cry tears of compassion for someone else, but not for me. Why?

1) I believe people are upholding me in prayer.
2) I have a conviction in my heart that I am fulfilling the purposes of God here.

His grace has sustained me from the start. It is easier to live in here now than it was to live outside with the uncertainty of my future. My total submission to the Lord is tested now. When I see His purpose and fruit in my life in here, I win!!

I have this inexplicable joy that defies logic. I've had the occasional frustration that left me angry, defiant and then temporarily sulky, but I am the winner overall.

Medication:

Medication is delivered to the unit three times a day. I require a tablet just once a day. When we are given medication we are to line up with our plastic glasses half filled with water. We must show our fingers putting our medication into our mouths, swallow the water, then open our mouths wide, and lift our tongues for an officer to inspect.

It reminds me of the movie, *"One Flew over the Cuckoo's Nest."* Some of the women take medicine to help with their drug withdrawals and may transfer the pill or liquid into someone else's mouth as a payment for something.

Such oral practices are not permitted in here.

As per the movie, we seem to have our very own Nurse Ratchet. This woman is a really grumpy, plump, middle-aged "sourpuss." Her mouth seems permanently held in the position that most resembles the rear of a cat. I'm always as polite as I can be, but one day, she was so rude to me that an officer actually told me not to worry about her.

My humiliations were not quite complete...

I picked up a persistent, barking cough from the watch-house conditions. To add to my indignities, my pelvic floors were not coping as well as they would normally, and I needed something to suppress the coughing. I was too embarrassed to go to the male officer in the fishbowl and explain why I needed to access my cell.

"Don't you do your pelvic floor exercises?" Nurse "Ratchet" demanded in a loud, accusing voice.

"Well yes, but I did give birth to *twins* and this cough isn't helping..."

She spoke to me as if I were an idiot and as if my answer was "back-chatting." I did get a bit testy as I hate poor customer service. I didn't appreciate my personal matters being ridiculed in front of everyone either. But in here I am not a customer. I am not an equal. I must be subservient, and accept disrespect from staff, if I am to survive. It's hard for a self-respecting person to tolerate such treatment.

I speak to the staff the same way I would if I were dealing with people from another business. We are incarcerated, however, in theory; we are still supposed to be treated with manners. Some officers do, and the women usually respond in kind. However, many do not; yet it is not our place to point out when a staff member is falling short. We have the right to complain, but few do unless the matter is really serious.

"I expected the women to be mean; but a nurse is simply doing a job, why would she bother being snide?" I complained to the Lord.

Hmmm. Time for an "Attitude" test.

I began praying for this horrible woman. I am sure she is lovely to those who matter to her. She is probably a sweet grandmother. Perhaps she just hates her job. So I prayed for

God's blessing on every area of her life. Then the Lord showed me a Scripture.

> "That which you do to the least of these brothers and sisters of mine, you do to me."

See Matthew 25:31-46 for the full context. It also warns,

> "That which you did *not* do for the least of these, you did *not* do for *Me*."

I felt the Lord ask me, "Who are the 'least' in society?"

"I think it's us, Lord," I answered. "People feel sorry for abused children, the handicapped, the sick, and the mentally ill; but we are despised."

"That's right, and yet she serves you."

The irony was not lost on me.

God has a great sense of humour!

What was funnier was when I shared my revelation with the nurse the next day! There is a part of me that is a little cheeky about the things of God, and I wanted to see her response.

How could I not?

As she served me, I thanked her politely and said, "You know the Bible says when you are serving us, you are serving Jesus."

She looked stunned, "Well, I don't believe that!"

I smiled at her and replied, "It doesn't matter if you believe it. We are the very least in society. What anyone does to us, they do to Christ. Thank you."

"Move along, Jenkins!" I'm sure the supervising officer was hiding a smile.

Perhaps the Lord will touch her, and perhaps not. It's not my call.

Sometime later, I was called to the Medical Centre to have another box "ticked." ("Box-ticking" is the term I use to describe pointless activities that provide "proof" of fulfilment of their "duty-of-care" obligation). *It doesn't mean issues are addressed properly.*

The doctor was actually quite nice. He spoke kindly and I shared my revelation about "the least among you," with him. This time he was surprised; but pleased.

"I try to do my best," he said. I offered to pray for him, and he accepted. There at his desk I took his hand and prayed for God to move in his life. He was touched and thanked me.

Fortunately, no officer could see us. What a strange tableau we would have made!

Out in the yard I noticed a young girl with a Bible. She sat quietly, on the end of the bench, and opened it. I smiled to myself. 'How nice,' I thought. Then, as I watched, she turned to the back pages, which I noticed had been snipped in lengths. Then it dawned on me. She was not looking up the concordance. I laughed at myself as she tore off one of the lengths and filled it with tobacco, making an improvised cigarette! 'Well it's the right paper for it!' I thought wryly.

Two chaplains came through like a refreshing stream. They prayed for anyone who wanted prayer. I was surprised at how many did. One of them promised to call my family, because my phone account was not yet connected.

Chaplains have since been advised they are not permitted to contact families on behalf of the inmates.

Amanda and I stuck together for support. We had to share a cell and, while we'd have preferred having our own, it was good to be there for one another.

S9 – Secure Block 9

First Letter to the outside world

Sunday, 1st February, 2009.

Dear Friends,

I hope you are all happy. I am having the most amazing time. I was moved to a new unit called S9; the last was S7, for Inductees. To go straight to S9 is a compliment. The next stage is "Residential," where there is more independence and freedom.

S9 holds thirty to forty women. The first day was a bit hard as the atmosphere was different, and some of the women had aggressive "attitudes." We were being sized up, assessed. Would they deign to talk to us? Finally, I was asked my name. A rough-looking lady with no front teeth let me watch her play cards with her two Aboriginal friends. I felt quite secure. *I figured this woman was about twelve years older than me. I later learned she is about five years younger. Hard living eventually shows on your face.*

There was one particularly vicious young woman (She was very dark, but not Aboriginal; African, I think), who seemed coiled to explode at any minute. She most accurately represented what I had expected to encounter. She was so full of anger that she seemed "possessed." I don't know how long she had been there. The next day she gave an officer a "mouthful" of abuse and was removed to the D.U. (Detention Unit). The tone of the unit changed to a more normal, relaxed one.

They are all very interested in what each other is in for. When it comes to fraud, most are single parents who did not declare extra earnings or claimed multiple pensions. Some were embezzlers. I wondered how many were quietly doing their time until they were able to access their "nest egg."

One or two women are so experienced in the court system, that they help other women understand various legal documents they

48

received. I was quite impressed with this. One in particular, was as smart as any lawyer on various legal topics. "When you see your lawyer, tell him to say this..." The only difference between her and a real lawyer was her compassion, and of course, her fee structure!

I met an old lady, a pensioner whose husband had done casual gardening for cash. By the time they were "dobbed in," the money he earned reached the amount punishable by prison. Both of them received four month sentences. In addition, once released, the pension they couldn't live on before will be docked until the money they were overpaid is paid back.

This poor, respectable grandmother was a broken woman. There was nothing I could say to comfort her. I wondered if her children could have helped support them. I wondered, 'could a local church be the family they needed, to help them?'

I wondered if those who are quick to judge are just as quick to refuse the discount of a "cash job," when they want something done...?

"To permit is to participate."

Tonight we had roast chicken which was surprisingly good. *I later discovered, the quality of the meals would vary, as the prison kitchen-workers came and went.* Lining up for meals reminds me of youth camps, where we'd line up, and someone would ladle various dishes onto our plates. Afterwards, we'd wash our plates, in water that was probably filthy by the time our turn came. Good times...

The second day, Amanda and I prayed hard, and bound a "spirit of strife," among other things. It was a much better day. I discovered six other Christians, one of whom, Sandra, is studying for a bachelor's degree in Ministries.

It seemed strange to me that such a high proportion of believers seemed to have so little impact. Over the following months, I met many Christians. I discovered they mostly keep to themselves, too ashamed to share their faith. Often these Christians had found faith as they struggled with an addiction. Through an outreach program, such as Drug Arm, they were loved and supported in churches.

Sometimes they still had outstanding warrants for which they were jailed. Sometimes they simply "fell off the wagon." One of them told me prison was the best thing for them or they would never have left the drug culture and found Christ. Other Christians I met were single mothers who defrauded Centrelink (welfare) by having cash jobs on the side.

Shame will cripple a person's effectiveness more than anything else. The difference for me was that I had a strong sense of destiny. If I hid my faith, I would not be true to myself and I would be rendered ineffective, and my prison time would serve no purpose.

Today, some women wanted to do a Bible study and asked me to lead it. It may sound strange but in this tense, rough place, to sit around a table with scripture is like an oasis. It refreshes us, and the atmosphere changes. I chose Matthew 18: 21-35 and taught on overcoming unforgiving attitudes.

Funnily enough, the others left the room, and before long some started acting up outside. Prayer stirs up both positive and negative responses, spiritually. *If someone blames God for their situation, they can be angered by seeing someone pray.* I warned the guard that we'd had a prayer meeting and that it could upset the spiritual climate. *In hindsight, that was probably better left unsaid.*

It's strange how quickly we can change the atmosphere by taking authority over it in prayer. It started as an argument among the women, over use of the phone, and then became an angry flare up. It could be that the music is turned up too loud "just for this song," and it causes irritation. Sometimes, there is no reason, other than someone wanting to assert herself.

Some of the women think I am a bit odd; but that's OK. I'm not quite "S4" material.

The next day, we had a chapel service. It was soothing to just bask in the corporate presence of God. What a relief to worship freely among believers! The chaplain used to be in a rock band. During worship, I began to intercede for the women here and wept for them. It was the first time I cried, since before my sentencing. I didn't even cry during the six days in that horrid watch-house.

At the end of the service I was given the opportunity to speak. I took the microphone and shared how I was a P.K. (Pastor's Kid), no better than they were. A lot of money and prayers had been invested to keep me out of jail, and yet the Lord brought me in.

My focus had been on selfish me. Now I am content and happy to offer whatever prayer and words of comfort, as people need them. I invited the ladies to seek me out to talk or pray. They were very responsive.

I am where the Lord wants me. I am in "the zone."

When we returned to the unit, I immediately saw the atmosphere was different. There was a more gentle tone and I know it was because we took charge in the spirit. I was not, and I'm still not, afraid. In fact, I feel like I am in charge, spiritually. The girls seem to respect me.

I told God I wanted to be effective and that is what is happening.

There is a lovely Aboriginal lady here who lives in Brownsville, normally. Could you ask Ps Larry if she can go there and be nurtured when she leaves? I have recommended it to her she really loves God.

In letters, I would occasionally ask for "someone" to tell a pastor, from a specific area, to be on the lookout for a referral of mine. Unfortunately a general request was not effective.

I discovered this in an embarrassing way, when I caught up with one of those pastors at a conference, after getting out:

"Hi Larry, it's good to see you again."

"Yes. Good to see you too."

"Have you had the Aboriginal women I referred, come along?"

"Oh yes, we have a lot of them."

"I met some lovely ones, while I was away."

"That's good." (Polite interest)

"Yes, I am so glad you are there to help them. Did Edna come and see you?"

"Edna? No I don't think so."

"Oh well. She and the others live in your area. They really touched my life."

He looked confused.

"You know I've been away?"

"A missions trip?" He still looked confused.

I blushed. "I... I was I jail" I whispered. "I thought you knew!"

"No I didn't. Wow." Uncomfortable pause.

"Yes, and I met a lot of Aboriginal women, some of whom I recommended your church to."

"Oh. Well. Thanks, that's great. Don't worry; if they turn up we'll look after them."

"Great, gotta go, see you."

You know that awkward feeling when you are talking with someone, and realise you are each having a different conversation? I felt like I had just realised I'd forgotten to put pants on.

Argh! I was going to have to sound people out before dropping the "J" word (Jail).

First Letter continued:

Funny Story: Sitting bored in the yard, a dominant woman piped up with, "Did you know that the armpit hair of the hand you write with is bigger than the other side?" "No! Yes! No!" they exclaimed, and then started darting around inspecting one another's armpits, to compare the size of the shaved areas! It was very funny to watch!

Please tell Jan that I received her card. If you make a card that has things glued or stuck on, it won't get through. People might have drugs under the stickers, which can be peeled off and licked.

If I work the pay rate ranges from $2.11 to $4.11 per day, I have put my name down to study a few topics. I'll do whatever becomes available. Those without work receive $9.27 per week; out of which all personal items must be purchased with the exception of sanitary products and meals.

Some women have no family to put money in their trust accounts. They must use the prison allowance to make phone calls, buy toothpaste, hair products, or even underwear once the prison issued three pairs have worn out.

Proper cigarettes are expensive, so the women buy pouches of tobacco. Most women smoke; therefore, tobacco and the accompanying "Tally Ho" papers are a priority here. They are a form of (illegal) currency.

Our day goes like this:

6.30 a.m. Awakened by an officer's voice coming through a speaker.

7.05 a.m. Officer looks in the window to see if you are still there, bedding must be folded with the mattress against the wall.

7.30 a.m. Stand by our door to be counted. We make sure our brown paper bag containing our crockery and cutlery is out with us. We will not be able to access our room (cell) until the afternoon lockdown at 1 p.m. If we want to be able to read or write, we take those materials out now too.

Breakfast: We can help ourselves to cereal, and bread for toasting, most of the day.

The yard door is open for the smokers and those who need to ring their children before the extended or foster family takes them off to school.

Any time after this, the medication trolley comes along. Sometimes it is accompanied by a normal, nice nurse, or sometimes by cranky nurse "Cats bum." (Referring to the pursed lips of her disdainful expression.)

9 a.m. Some go to work. Work could be gardening, cutting up rags in a workshop, or working in the kitchen.

Seven people are allowed to go to the gym or the library. These activities often clash, even though they are not offered every day.

I haven't been to the library yet; but we can go twice a week for ten minutes.

I learned to put my name down for the library trip very early. Some officers would let you do this; others would not take your name until closer to the time. I chose to risk their annoyance rather than miss out.

Sometimes a chapel service will be scheduled. On those days we didn't know whether an officer would permit only seven to go or follow the rules which didn't have a restricted number. This inconsistency became a matter of contention down the track.

12.00 p.m. Lunch

1.00 p.m. We can go to our room, or stay in the hall, or yard.

2.15 p.m. Leave our cell. We have to stay in the hall or yard; it can be very boring. Sometimes we are allowed to be locked in our cell again.

4.30 p.m. Dinner and last minute smoke time.

6.15 p.m. Locked back in our cells. I still share with Amanda, which is good. We alternate who sleeps on the floor.

You can't send me any books. It takes a while for mail to arrive, because it has to be read by a staff member. Nice when it does though. God is good.

One girl thought I was a junkie at first, because I am so pale. "No." I stretched out my arms. "Check out these beautiful veins, bet you wish you had them."

She reached forward, grasped my wrist in one hand, and tapped my forearm professionally with the other, "Yep, good veins!"

I went to an art class today. I'm not great at art. Some of the Indigenous girls do beautiful Aboriginal paintings. I don't know where they find the patience to do all those dots. Perhaps it's relaxing. Some of their work is just breathtaking.

I met another chaplain today. She said she came to find me as the other chaplains had told her about me. She prayed for me, and then I prayed for her and the other chaplains. She was surprised and touched.

You can send an email to Justin, and he will print it out and send it with his mail, if you would like to write.

Bye for now

Love, Trish

Journal notes

No date

Some of the girls asked me to "speak in tongues," as they had heard me doing it. I didn't want to turn it into a party trick, so I said, "I'll only do it when I have something to pray for. Is there something you'd like me to pray for?"

"Yes, OK. Pray for my mother who is sick."

"Alright, give me your hand."

It was a supernatural moment, when the anointing passed from me into the other woman.

She felt it.

I felt it.

I'm sure the other women sensed it.

I am not afraid. In fact, I feel a subtle authority. The women seem to respect me. I am very discreet about my prayer language as it can freak people out. It's just supernatural enough for them to take me seriously.

There is a retarded woman who has occasional outbursts. I heard she was a prostitute, and got caught hosing herself clean in someone's backyard. She seems to have the mind of an unpredictable six year old, easily angered and upset. Even the really tough girls treated her with kid gloves.

Every now and then she is taken away to S4, the mental unit. I don't know why she isn't in a secure mental hospital.

I went to art class as an interesting diversion. Unfortunately, I'm just as bad at art as I always was. There were several requests from women in the unit for me to steal coloured paper; but I refused. I didn't think they were serious, until I observed paper being secreted at a rapid rate, when the supervisor's back was turned!

It occurred to me that some of these women would be very adept shop-lifters!

We are supposed to line up with our plates for dinner, but often one woman will line up with a lot of plates. When you think you are third in line, you could be twelfth! The woman in front loads up her friends' plates, while we wait. When I asked what was going on, another woman got right in my face and demanded to know if I had a problem with it!

One of the officers uses foul language and makes derogatory remarks. He decided to play a game where the "last person in their cell for the evening would have their TV switched *off*, and they would have to choose another person to have the same done!"

It didn't happen. I suppose he thought it was funny; I just saw it as an abuse of power. Not everyone thinks about what goes on, they just accept it.

I think about everything that happens.

One of the pregnant women is unpopular with her dining table group. They made her cry; it saddens me that women would do that to one another. She is too frightened to complain.

Of course, this meant I deliberately made friends with her.

Some women try to control who is friends with whom, who people can talk to, who must be ignored.

It took me a while to "twig" to this because those kinds of hints go over my head. I talk to whomever I want. That includes the pregnant girl.

I don't seem to get picked on which surprises me in one way; but not in another.

2nd Letter

8th February

Hello to my dear friends,

Things are happening. I've had a rather dramatic Sunday morning. We had a chapel service. It was lovely, based on Philippians 4:13, "I can do all things through Him who strengthens me."

The lady chaplain asked for some testimonies of how God has answered their prayers.

An Aboriginal woman raised her hand, "I was being raped with a stick. Then I called out the name of Jesus and the man hurting me ran away."

Another young woman testified that as a little girl she had been hurt by a paedophile every day for four years. One day she prayed for God's angels to make him go away and all of a sudden, he got dressed and left! That young woman gave her heart to the Lord this morning.

I shared about praying for our unit. One woman objected to my having prayed for my unit; then I explained that I pray good things for everyone and gave examples, such as for good health and peace of mind. I might have been better off staying silent; however, I wanted to encourage the women to pray for a good atmosphere in their units.

It was risky because people have all sorts of opinions about prayer. They sometimes blame God for their problems, and can resent people who love Him.

I also asked the group to pray for a particular officer as he was often really cranky. I made the mistake of using his name. That was to get me in big trouble later.

Sandra is in for GBH (Grievous Bodily Harm), among other things, and I've been helping her with her Bachelor of Ministry studies. She gave a testimony about her husband forcing her into prostitution to get drugs. Although still in prison, she is free on the inside. She is very brave, because she is often mocked by other women for her past. Broken people often feel the need to denigrate others. Perhaps it mistakenly makes them feel superior.

Some of them were sniggering in the back row. To my annoyance the officer did nothing to quiet them. Perhaps she was sniggering on the inside herself? *Hmm.* I mentally added her to my prayer list.

Anyway, Sandra asked if she could pray for the young woman who was abused, as she had led her to the Lord, back in the unit. She also asked me to assist. I looked to the chaplain, who nodded.

Not being one to waste an opportunity, I asked if anyone else needed prayer for healing, broken hearts or relationships; if it was OK with the chaplain. "Yes" was her answer.

I warned the group that things can happen when we pray. Well they did. God turned up and it looked like "demons" manifested. The woman I was praying for was very large. Obesity is a huge problem in prison (pardon the pun), due to the lack of activity available. My ministry student friend stood behind and the woman was "slain in the Spirit." In other words, she was so touched by God; she literally fell to the ground. It's not easy to explain. Imagine an energy flowing through a person that the person they touch can feel or sense. Sometimes it makes them drop to the floor.

Another woman had arms so scarred from self-harm; they looked like a tractor tire had run over them. She also collapsed, when I prayed for her. Then she arose smiling, free and happy. If you think it sounds weird, imagine how it looked!

As we left I saw the officer speaking to the chaplain, and I knew she was in trouble. I apologised to the officer, although I'm not sure what for; because I didn't want the chaplain to get into trouble.

The officer said the prayer made some of the women unsettled. I explained that a normal "traditional" service doesn't have much impact. I said the Holy Spirit upsets their "demons."

Instead I should have said "the Holy Spirit touches the issues these women bring with them and there can be a reaction." The officer admitted she thought our prayers had made a difference to our unit.

After the service some of the women who were "unsettled" reported me for making someone fall down when I prayed. It freaked them out. I was in trouble big time. I was summoned to the block Supervisor's office.

He yelled at me, going on and on, about not forcing my beliefs on anyone else. How that demand fit into a chapel service made no sense to me. He went apoplectic when he talked about "laying on hands" anywhere, especially in our unit. I was not to "force my religion down anyone's throat." *Such a tired phrase! It was a chapel service for goodness sake!*

He threatened me with S1, where the trouble-makers go, if I offered prayer and words of comfort or encouragement in the unit. It wasn't my place or my business…

I remained calm. I told him I only prayed for people who wanted to be prayed for. *I wanted to suggest that I was the one being forced to listen to other people's beliefs via their profanity; but I figured being argumentative would not help my position.*

He told me I was banned from "praying in tongues." I wasn't sure that suppression of my faith was allowed; but I wasn't going to challenge him. He said I was definitely **not** to get anyone "saved." I could only pray alone in my cell, quietly.

He was also mad that I had named an officer for prayer. That officer was in the room. I agreed that I shouldn't have, and apologized; *although I couldn't quite put my finger on why. I wish I had the courage to ask him to explain why it was wrong.*

It felt weird. I was listening and watching what appeared like a movie unfolding. Could I seriously be standing here in a prison being berated for my faith? For expressing faith in a chapel service! Why offer a chapel service at all? Is it merely to satisfy the "box ticking," system? Is this a third-world or Eastern-bloc country? Is this what the Bible refers to as being persecuted for my faith?

As he spoke I felt honoured that I was living what the Bible talks about, being persecuted for Christ's sake. Many responses ran through my head, some very witty; but none of which would have gone over well. I could have been defensive; but I decided to leave it with God, and just do the "Yes sir, no sir, three bags full sir."

The supervisor asked me what I was in for. I told him I'd been caught up in a scam and did the wrong thing; but I didn't actually steal any money.

"Well, were you praying *then*?" He asked scornfully. "Obviously not enough!" I smiled wryly.

"Get out! If I hear you are laying hands on anyone or praying outside your cell, you will be banned from chapel for a month!"

"Goodness me," I replied in dismay. "I have been trying to show how good I am so you would send me to 'Residential.'"

"Residential is a very good idea." he said. Perhaps I will be sent there sooner now. *It was not to be.*

Please pray for the Supervisor.

Gotta love irony!

Prior to the visit to the Supervisor, I'd had to report to the health bay. I waited with another young woman who said she was from S1. She looked so sad. "Did you do something bad?" I asked gently. My eyes widened when she said, "Yeah, fighting, and I am banned from going to chapel."

Banning her from chapel? How stupid and small-minded to think chapel is just an "activity," a privilege to be revoked. Chapel is what she needed. I believe the only people who should be banned from chapel are the mockers.

She said she keeps hurting herself.

I asked, "Do you believe in God? She answered, "I believe there is something; but I don't really know what."

My heart was touched by her simplicity. She was a "cutter." I got a "Word of Knowledge" about her past and some other matters. I already knew cutters were usually victims of sexual abuse. I told her, "God loves you very much."

She asked how I knew certain things about her. I told her God had just let me know. I asked if she would like me to pray for her and she said 'oh, yes please!'

Remember, this was before I was banned from offering prayer.

A chaplain gave me two Christian books to read. She had rung Mum and had a great chat. The chaplain and I talked about how my being here is part of God's plan. He works all things together for good for those who love Him. This is turning out for "good." I can't write all the details of what happened in this letter, but will have lots of stories when I return.

Chaplains are appreciated by the women; but are treated with little respect by officials here. Having them merely provides a "tick in the box" under "services" offered. One day we were all shut down in our cells and the chapel service, scheduled for later that day was cancelled. Nobody notified the chaplain who had driven from across town at her own expense. Not being staff equals not important.

If only they knew how grateful they should be to these volunteers. If only they knew how chaplains keep women from tumbling over the edge and causing serious problems.

One young woman, who has a mocking spirit, pretends to be a Christian. I can tell she's faking. One of the "bad" girls told me to be careful, as a lot of the women have mental problems and they may cause trouble for me. I need a lot of discernment. If the unstable ones get stirred up, it causes trouble for everyone.

I spent a pleasant twenty minutes having a "cuppa" with the young woman who cautioned me. She seemed to care, and I appreciated her concern for me. She herself has a bi-polar disorder and can be violent, but I like her.

I built a deep friendship with this woman. It saddens me that society has no place for her.

I still carry this warm, fulfilled feeling around in my chest. I have been doing God's work; but it's now time to change tack.

"The effectual fervent (not necessarily loud) prayers of a righteous woman availeth much." (James 5:16 paraphrased for context)

I sent Justin a photo of me smiling in my uniform. I want our children to see mummy looking happy.

Thank you for your letters and cards, I have a shoe box I keep them in.

A few of the women want to read "Bad Girls of the Bible," after I have finished it. They are very interested in "bad girls," like themselves.

I want you to all know I am doing OK. I miss and love you all. I know that God has a plan and purpose for my life.

I contact Justin and our daughters by phone every day. They are living with Mum and Dad. Please pray for Justin and our children, especially for Chelsea. It is very hard for her as she is now ten and wants to protect the twins. They still have not been cleared to visit so I don't have any visits except from the chaplain.

Until next time

Love, Trish

Journal notes

No date

The hypocrisy of a system that prevents a person from expressing their faith in a *chapel* service is beyond belief. Would they interfere with a Muslim worshipping Allah even though it made other prisoners uncomfortable?

My faith doesn't fit into their checklist. You can have faith here as long as it isn't real, as long as it doesn't actually work. To expect God to show up is against the rules. To have Him *actually* show up is to cause trouble. It reminds me of the cartoon of Jesus sitting on some church steps, saying to someone, "Don't worry, they won't let me in either!"

Christians are allowed to be "nice," as long as they are not effective.

Ironically, the church never prospered more than when it was repressed.

How sad that material prosperity often makes Christians fat and complacent, concerned more with the preservation of their comfort than standing up for the weak.

Well, at least I wasn't being bashed up like Christian prisoners in Russia and China! No. Here I was simply a victim of the politically correct culture where every view is accepted and protected except a Christian one.

I find it hilarious that he had no idea of the advantage he'd given me! By threatening me, he actually gave me more credibility among the women!

There was much interest on my return to the unit, along with unrest among the women. A controlling woman had instructed some of the others not to talk to me. One refused and spent all afternoon with me.

Well, so much for keeping a low profile...

The funny thing is that I was able to use what happened. Several women asked me what happened. I answered "I'm not

64

allowed to pray for anyone, I'm not allowed to mention Jesus or talk about God. I am not allowed to pray in my prayer language. They are scared it will freak people out too much."

"Well, *that's* religious persecution, they can't do that!"

"Yeah, I know; but what can you do?" I shrugged. "They are the ones with the power."

"Yeah, #%&*ing #$%&*s."

I felt a shift in the atmosphere after that. If anything, more women asked me to pray with them. Somehow they sensed I carried a kind of power.

I don't carry any power of my own; but I carry something.

3rd Letter

10th February

Hello to my dear friends,

I am in good spirits. After Sunday's "kafuffle," I decided to keep a low profile, just reading and writing.

I prayed for a long time about how to respond to what happened and the Lord just said, "Do nothing, let me handle it." Hard for me; but it was too serious for me to interfere.

I heard from today's guards that what caused the biggest concern was "making that lady fall down." They said if she had been hurt, I would have been in big trouble.

Do you know what it's like trying to explain how the Holy Spirit can move through a 60kg (130lb) woman and cause a 200kg (440lb) woman to collapse on the ground? I could have been sent to S1 where the really bad ones go, or worse, to S4 where the mentally defective women go. Then there is the DU or "Discipline Unit," known in the movies as "The Hole," for punishment.

Anyway, I prayed for God to handle it all.

On Monday one of the women who complained about me was sent to health bay, while her girlfriend was taken to S4. The girlfriend was one who had only spoken to me, to say how much she hated me and all "Poshies!" I told her I didn't feel that way about her and left it at that. Now she is gone.

Some new girls came in today from S7. One of them said "Hey, you prayed with me in the other unit for my son!"

"Shhh" I said. "I'm not allowed to talk about Jesus, unless you ask... so feel free to ask, OK?"

"OK" she answered, "I sure will." She smiled.

The Milk Story:

During the first week in S9, my cell-mate, Amanda, was being picked on whenever I was not near her. She was hassled over her place in the line for the phone and had nasty things said to her in passing.

To make matters worse, Amanda had her milk stolen twice. We are each issued a 600ml carton (about 20oz) at lunchtime each day. Our cell number is written on them and they all go in one fridge in the kitchen.

I was mad that Amanda had lost her milk two days in a row. I knew the spiritual force behind these women would not pick on me, because I am strong. However, I was not putting up with this. I prayed and considered my options. Telling an officer was out of the question.

I joked about how surprising it was to discover a thief in prison. I knew before long that all twenty-nine women would know of my displeasure. I asked the Lord what to do and I believe I received instruction.

Reaching for a marker, I wrote the words "SPAT IN," next to the cell number on each of our milk cartons. The funny thing is, a little later someone called my bluff.

"You did not spit in your milk did you?"

"I'm not saying," I answered primly. She looked hard at me and announced "No, you didn't!"

Hmm, action required. Calmly I opened the fridge, reached for my milk, opened the top and deliberately dropped some spittle into it, while staring the girl down. I then just as calmly put it back.

"Eew, that's disgusting!"

"Yeah, well nobody is going to take our milk again are they?" I walked away, knowing it would take less than 1 minute for the event to buzz around.

Amanda and I spent the evening praying the Word and blessing our antagonists. The next day was a new day and the "bitchy" spirit was gone.

If only I'd had the same guts in high school. It certainly felt like grade nine!

Library

We are allowed to go to the library twice a week. Yesterday was my first time. I couldn't wait to go! To be in a room filled with rows of books was Heaven! Granted there weren't many but the smell was the same. I inhaled deeply and closed my eyes.

'This is my territory,' I thought. 'Here, I am normal.' At the end of each row was a chair. I sat in the chair in the last row and soaked in the wonderful feeling and scent of being surrounded by books.

For a few precious minutes, I pretended I was a normal person in a library, somewhere outside these walls.

God is so good. I managed to borrow the book, *"I Was Wrong,"* by Jim Bakker. I can relate to some of the things he wrote about prison and the shame he felt. I am thrilled that God placed that book just where I would find it in the ten minutes we were allotted to be there.

Fear not, I am OK and I am not feeling sad. Please pray that my close friends from the watch-house and I all go over to "Residential" soon. One of them says she will believe in God, if that happens!

Love you all so much.

Trish Jenkins

4ᵗʰ Letter

12ᵗʰ February

My dear family and friends,

The news is dominated by images of bushfire-ravaged Victoria. The women here are just as shocked and saddened as anyone outside. We are participating in a walk-a-thon on Saturday to help the bushfire appeal.

Don't worry, I'm not asking for sponsorship money! I don't need much money here anyway. We were told that if we donate from our own trust accounts we could walk around the grounds for one hour.

We have lovely grass and fragrant flowering bushes.

Instead we were locked in a fenced sports field to walk in circles in the sun for the hour. It also meant I missed chapel because they were delayed in getting us out. Anyway, it was for a good cause.

The sports field never gets used for sport. Apparently it's too hard to supervise. If there is a fight at the far end, too much violence can be done before officers can get there to break it up.

We are not allowed on the grass. *Sometimes I reach out and plucked a fragrant flower and kept it with me. It smelled like freedom.*

We walk instead, on concrete paths from one building to the next. Some blades have managed to push their way up between the concrete floor and wall of our caged yard (pen). I like to sit and feel these.

I told some of the girls I was desperate to roll on the grass so I picked a few gallant blades, dropped them on the concrete under the basketball hoop and laid down, rolling on them from side to side! It made them laugh.

I remembered the young woman I'd met who claimed to be a firebug. She was just fascinated by fire. She was also a drug addict and had a wild, crazed look in her eyes.

Such people are unable to think ahead to consequences. It's as though they became retarded at a particularly immature stage. As such, it is difficult for them to have compassion for others. Their life is all about satisfying their immediate desires, whether it is drugs, sex, or an outburst of profanity.

A lady asked me why God would let those bushfires rage out of control and kill so many. The best answer I had was, "I don't know." I could point her to books about "Apologetics" and I could talk about the Fall of Man and Grace; but the truth is we are really only guessing, and a guess does not provide comfort.

Sinners do sinful things. Sin is separation from God so why blame God? He didn't start the blazes. However, He expects His people to do something about them. The best I can do is share God's love and his desire to be part of our lives; but He won't intrude if we ignore him.

One poor lady has a daughter who gave birth at the age of fifteen to a stillborn baby. Now at sixteen, she is about to give birth again. She needs her mum; but isn't speaking to her. She is angry at her mother for being stupid enough to drive unlicensed and get locked up. Like her own choices have been so smart? So many poor decisions result in great pain.

On a lighter note, I have been practicing my French with a black French girl. She was caught at the airport with 2kg of heroin in the soles of her platform shoes. The officials told her if she had been caught during her Hong Kong stopover, she would have been executed!

This girl comes from a sheltered Catholic family, and has a toddler back in France. Her father is so angry he won't talk to her. She knew no English before being imprisoned. She mostly keeps to herself.

I made her laugh with my tale of working at Dreamworld back in the 1990's. Each year for two weeks, we were inundated with French speaking New Caledonians. I ran the Old Time Photo shop which then backed onto the photo-lab. I was often called on to interpret.

One particular time, the photo lab had accidentally destroyed a lady's film. This was before digital cameras were widely used. I was called in to explain the situation to the lady and to apologise for them.

"Bonjour," I began.

"Bonjour" she replied.

" 'Je parle français un pur' (I speak a little French.)"

"Ah, bon, bon! (Good, good)" she replied.

"D'accord, (Ok). Le film…"

Lady: "Ouis, ouis."

"Le machine," I used my hands to describe the film going into the machine. "Je regret…"

Then I slammed my hands together several times like I was screwing something up and growled, "Aah…Arragh…Arrgh Arrgh!"

"Ooh la la!" She cried.

"Oui, ooh la la!" I cried. "Non film!"

The photo lab girls stared at me, somewhat stunned.

"We could have done that!"

"Oui, but it wouldn't have been as entertaining!"

My new French friend laughed out loud and agreed to help me improve my language skills.

I have been given permission to buy a hair colour. We are expected to maintain our appearance, as per their records, and to make us easier to identify should we abscond. The day before court I had my foils done by a new hairdresser. Unfortunately, I couldn't get the colour I needed.

One "blonde" girl here has dark re-growth six inches long! I saw my future *look* a few months down the track.

It won't be pretty...

We have a uniform which is a blue polo shirt, grey shorts, and sports crop-top for a bra. Footwear is thongs (flip flops) or socks and sneakers. My crop-top was riding a bit high the other day and a girl pointed out, I had put it on backwards! How embarrassing. Of course, I had to say the old line "You know you are going to have a bad day when you accidentally put your bra on backwards - and it fits better!"

Today we are waiting for our "buy up" order. We put a form in on Sundays for things like toiletries, snack food, stationary and tobacco. Fortunately, I don't smoke; though most of the women do. I decided to order some tobacco and keep it for when they run out. It will buy me a lot of favours and, since I can't talk about the Lord, it is one way to bless them. Yes, I know it's bad. The body is a temple; but tobacco is something they value highly and there are very few other comforts here for them.

I didn't realise at the time that what I did was a serious breach. All incoming and outgoing mail is supposed to be read by prison staff. By telling you in a letter, I could have been found out. However, it's likely that not every word, of everyone's letters, gets monitored.

We can order from a newsagent each fortnight, so I was able to get some gel pens and a puzzle book to help pass the time. We do the puzzles in pencil and then rub it out, so we can share them around. Such little gestures build relationships between strangers. The women know I am not allowed to talk about the Lord first, so they ask me about Him and church, and why I am not bitter and depressed. It really touches me.

I am currently reading Jim Bakker's story. I recommend it to everyone, especially leaders. He was one of the many church leaders who fell during the late 1980's, early 1990's. As he details his prison experience I can relate to some of it. One of the anxieties I anticipated was the body search. Some of the girls "bank" drugs in their body's personal "hiding place." Fortunately laws changed in the late 1990's, preventing the physical invasion of a woman's body.

My searches were not as graphic as Jim's. His courage in the face of repeated disappointments is a testimony to his faith. I cannot imagine the kind of sentence stretching ahead of me that he faced. You can cope with anything for a short time. Thank God his sentence was not the forty-five years originally given.

As I read Jim Bakker's book he mentions preachers I am familiar with: Mike Murdock, John Hagar and Kenneth Copland. Many had continued to encourage him, visit, and write to him. People like Chuck Colson, who went to prison for his role in the Watergate scandal, and then formed Prison Fellowship. Bakker made the point, "As long as we continue to try to defend our past or cling to our innocence, we are still being held hostage by prior events." I am no longer a hostage to my mistakes. Instead of keeping it a secret I want the church to know how easy it is to slip into using scripture to "deafen" ourselves to that which we don't want to hear."

One of my fears was losing the respect of the rest of the church. That was pride, and the Lord showed me I am not to be concerned about that. He also showed me that what I feared in others was actually in myself.

When the tele-evangelists began to fall, in the late 1980's, I was just as upset and angry as anyone. How could they do it? I was embarrassed as a Christian.

There is no need to feel that way. God is not embarrassed about how his bride looks. People are still hungry for God. We are supposed to restore those who fall in a spirit of humility, "There, but for the grace of God, go I."

I had fallen off my own pedestal. Even though many injustices happened, I still only have myself to blame.

I have had great compassion and understanding, when friends made poor choices; but somehow I had higher expectations for myself. Pride again.

Dear friends, God will do whatever it takes to get your attention. Both Jim Bakker and I had to be incarcerated, in order to reach a deeper level of communion with the Lord. I recommend you take the initiative, and chase Him so he doesn't have to try too hard to get your attention.

I have been shut down from sharing my faith and now I am concentrating on hearing from God. My most regular prayer is that I will be effective and that this experience is not wasted.

I have a joy that bubbles up continually. These women are so precious. I have asked Jesus to help me see these women through his eyes, and I think I'm starting to. "Where sin abounds, grace abounds more so," as per Romans 5:20. God is just so beautiful in here.

I got news this afternoon that Amanda and I should be going to the Helena Jones House at Albion next week. Helena Jones is a minimum-security communal house to help women integrate back into society. It also offers a lot more freedom and privileges. Thanks to those who have been praying for me.

Part of me does not want to leave these women. When I told them I was leaving, several came to hug me, and say how they will miss my cheeriness and the "strange things" I would say.

One informed me that I was moving quickly because I am a "stiff." She was giving me a compliment. There is no hiding my "straightness." For example, one time a couple of the drug addicts let me look at their arms close up.

"Oh, so *those* are track marks?" They had deep purple marks about an inch long all over their hands and arms. I turned out my lily-white arms again; I have always had good veins.

"Check out these babies; pure virgins!"

We all laugh at my straightness. I'm known as a "180-Straighty," in both sexual preference and lifestyle!

I sat in the concrete yard this evening, where most of the women sit, having their final smoke for the day. The air was filled with quiet chatter, punctuated with profanity that I scarcely noticed. *The Lord had answered my prayer that it be like "white-noise," in the background and unnoticed by my ears.*

My heart filled with love. I looked around, making eye contact with various ones, and they smiled back at me.

We were all here together. Drug addicts, bullies, lesbians, drunk and disqualified drivers, a grandmother pensioner whose husband had a cash job on the side, another old lady who told the police, the drugs they found were not her grandson's, but hers. Yeah right. Toothless, obese, skinny, gamblers, armed robbers, assault and battery perpetrators, women who'd killed their childhood molester, those on remand for murder, and others who've taken lives.

Somehow, they all had a beauty emanating from them. It was a warm, touching, supernatural feeling for me. They were all daughters of the King; princesses who didn't know it.

It's strange to feel this from people who are capable of terrible evil.

I hope I continue to see as Christ sees, long after I leave. I hope it takes less than prison for each of you to see the people around you the same way, no matter how "icky."

I have not felt this joy, satisfaction, and powerful anointing, in years. Can I say that all the rubbish I've been through was worth it, to get to this? If I had known what a blessed time I would have in here, I would not have suffered so much.

By the way, even though I can't talk about God, a lady asked me to help her write a letter to her uncle and aunt, who look after her children. She wanted to ask their forgiveness and beg to be able to see them.

I prayed and wrote a letter of humble repentance with her and explained God's grace and forgiveness. I then gave her Bronwyn Healy's book, "Trophy of Grace," from the library. I pointed out the salvation prayer at the back. She is ready to ask Jesus into her life.

Prison is proving to be one of the most exciting and satisfying times of my life.

Feel free to forward this letter to whomever you wish. Thanks again for all your prayers.

God bless,

Trish

5th Letter

14th February (Valentine's Day)

To my beloved family and friends

Last night I had a bit of an "Attitude." My ministry-student friend, Sandra, has been told she is not allowed to give anyone a Bible or other Christian books. It's not like she's giving them out to just anyone, these are women who have asked for material. Being a student, Sandra has access to more books than the library offers. In addition, the chaplains have been instructed that there are to be no hugs, no embraces when greeting us.

What a crock! The chaplains are dearly loved by the women here, even the ones who don't believe, simply because they care. If we have a serious complaint and we do not get any satisfaction at the unit level, we have a "Blue Letter" system. A "blue letter" is not a letter full of foul language. It's for delivering confidential complaints and to the General Manager.

I was getting mad and mentally composing such a "blue letter," in order to complain about religious discrimination. Then I felt the Lord say "Leave it to me."

So often in the past I have tried to "help" the Lord and made matters worse. Ever done that? Sigh. So instead I prayed for God's blessing on the administrators. I prayed that they would view the chaplains' work with favour.

Tomorrow we have chapel. The chaplain used to be in an Australian rock band. All the women who go to chapel, say they prefer the "full-gospel" style, as it is more real, more enjoyable, and they feel God.

No moving in the "gifts" of the Spirit is allowed, though, especially by me!

All day today, I have had great chats about God with girls who have shown no prior interest. One had attended a church in an outback mining town in North Western Queensland. She knew the same pastor there that I knew. I led her in a rededication prayer.

There are a number of backslidden Christians here. Somehow as teenagers they got off track. The Lord allows them to end up here, where they find their faith again.

I pray that families would be sincere in their faith, and youth workers continue to be effective; that drugs and jail are not necessary for our young ones, before they wake up.

Jim Bakker's book is long. I skipped much of the correspondence between him and his wife as their marriage was breaking up. I felt uncomfortable, like it was none of my business.

I so admire the man for his humility and honesty. I hope the Lord does powerful things through him and that the churches he visits are worthy of his "pearls."

One thing we both agree on is a changed perspective of prosperity. I couldn't "give a toss" about how much money I make when I get out, as long as I am EFFECTIVE. I have been more effective for Jesus in three weeks in prison, than I have in the last few years. It gives me a buzz that I can only compare to being in love. I'm sure much of it is thanks to your prayers sustaining me, and the lovely cards, and letters you have sent me.

I have no depression. I have a freedom and joy that I had previously only experienced in deep worship. God is moving here.

It's exciting to share my experiences here with you all as they happen. I'm not waiting until after my sentence is over to write about them; they are virtually coming to you LIVE!!

I finally have my own room (cell). I had been sharing with Amanda since the 22nd January, the day of my sentencing. Now on her own, she has read all of Matthew and Mark. She is praying the way I taught her, and is building her relationship with God. I have not yet got her baptised in the Holy Spirit. I am

78

not very confident about doing that. The "speaking in tongues" is a big deal in here, and a few of the girls would like to have that gift.

Imagine the trouble I'd be in, if half a dozen women started freaking the whole unit out by babbling in another tongue!

It sounds like something you would only read about in a book.

Please pray for an outpouring of the Holy Spirit that can't be mistaken for anything but God. I will be leaving my little flock in Sandra's hands, as I will shortly be transferred to the Helena Jones Centre at Albion. If you ever wondered who cooks "Meals on Wheels," for the elderly and infirm of Brisbane; the Helena Jones inmates, help prepare it.

I don't mind the prison food. It is better than hospital food and better than my cooking (though not as good as my mother's). The women look at me strangely, when I see what we are having and I murmur, "Oh yum!"

I've cut out bread from my diet and I don't eat between meals. Many do. There's not much to do so they eat. Consequently, many are obese.

When I got out I was sometimes asked about the food, and I would answer "tongue-in-cheek," "Well, bread and water can be problematic when you've cut out carbs..."

We read, we write letters and we talk. Some days we are allowed to go to the gym. Today I ran twenty-five laps of the indoor court, which is about 2km. As I ran my laps, I passed a young woman playing guitar. After I cooled down, I joined her and those surrounding her. They were trying to remember the words of a "Guns 'n' Roses" song.

I asked if she knew how to play "House of the Rising Sun." She did. Now don't get all religious on me, I know it's about a brothel; but I had an idea.

I sang the verses I could remember. I sounded better than I normally would, because of the acoustics of the shed that was our "gym." I then asked if they had heard "Amazing Grace" sung to the same tune.

"No."

Well off I went singing three verses and repeating the first one!

"Amayyyyy.........zinggrace......howsweeeeet.....thesounnnd ....thatsaved.....awretch......like me...eeeeeee....

They listened to the end.

It was a "Wow" moment.

One young woman was crying her eyes out. I hadn't met any of these girls before; but suddenly we hugged.

I told them the parable about "the sheep and the goats." I explained how we were considered the "least" in society; but Jesus values us so much that He said, "That which is done to the least of these, is being done to me." (Matthew 25:40, paraphrased). That's how much he cares for us in prison.

I encouraged them to come and hear the guy who was in the rock band, at chapel in the morning. There should be a good number.

You may be wondering how the tobacco I ordered went over. Well, some of them were astounded that I had bought tobacco when I didn't smoke. Some of the women didn't get their order filled so I was able to help them.

I decided the wisest move was to entrust my tobacco to a woman who was a natural leader, and whom I trusted to be fair, and she was. One or two of the women cautioned me against others who would try to "con" me, because I was so "nice."

Even the girl who had glared at me, and said, "I hate your guts," needed tobacco, and thanked me.

I wondered if the niceties would run out when the tobacco did; but there seems to be a different tone in the air now.

My gesture blew them away and broke down walls.

Sandra gave up smoking. She had none today and no cravings. She has been praying and getting "words" for people. She is very excited.

I found myself watching the children's programs, *"Diego"* and *"Dora the Explorer,"* this morning. I started tearing up as I imagined my daughters watching at the same time.

I love them so much. They are such happy little critters. I pray that they will not have "hang ups" from this trial we are going through as a family.

I am very grateful to those of you who have kept in contact with Mum and Dad and Justin. Also, to Ps Luke Harris and the "Citikidz" team; thanks for giving my daughters that extra love and attention. I am touched by the messages I have received from you.

If you are going through a trial that you have no control over, choose to do it God's way. You'll go through it anyway. Getting bitter or angry at the unfairness of it all is short-sighted.

Find God's perspective. If you can't find it, then choose to trust him anyway.

All things pass; and you can have access to everything you need to be able to cope, and cope well. You must resolve to go through it the way God would want you to.

I'll sign off now.

God bless you all.

Trish

6th Letter

18th February

Hello Church!

I have been working with the scripture, "Where sin abounded, grace abounded more so."

(Romans 5:20b).

Prison is a pretty intense "front line" for sin. Now I am finding that the Lord is answering my prayers, almost immediately.

For example, yesterday I hugged a friend and pecked the top of her head in a gesture of affection. She happens to be a lesbian, and her roommate exploded with foul language, telling me to "Go kiss someone else!" I just said, "No worries," and walked away. As has become my practice, I prayed God's blessing on her.

I suppose I should have known better. I wouldn't do it to someone else's husband or boyfriend. Still, it's hard to take lesbians seriously when you aren't one. I've known a few gay men and they are usually much more fun.

Amanda wisely reminded me *not* to tell the girl I was praying for her as I could get reported, or worse. Anyway, each time I saw her, or thought of her, I prayed for God to bless her.

Then, without warning, she came to me, put her arm on my back and apologised profusely, saying I can come and talk to her anytime. This is a girl I had not spoken to *once* in three weeks, as I just sensed I should leave her alone. God is so good.

Grace sure outweighs sin. I can see why churches under persecution thrive. We don't always hear about the joy that comes as we watch the dynamics unfold. God really is the master chess player.

I missed last Sunday's service, due to our walk-a-thon being postponed. I was told I would be back in time; but the "powers that be" decided to shuffle the times, so I missed out.

Most of the ladies in our unit went to the service and when they returned, they told me it was amazing. Nobody sat in the back scoffing. All stood to worship. Some came to me afterwards, demanding to know why they hadn't been able to stop crying!

Each day Sandra and I have led someone to Jesus, or ministered to them in a deep way. There are a number of Christians here; but they don't really stand out. They don't offer to pray for others.

I guess when you are "called," you can't help functioning in your gift. I knew I took a risk, when I decided to be open and not hide away; but I knew God had me here for a reason and I wanted to make the most of it.

Since I couldn't go to church, the chaplain, the visiting minister, and another lady came to see me. They laid hands on me and prayed in the Spirit. No one could hear us. I was touched by their thoughtfulness.

The chaplaincy is not well respected by the authorities here. They are very restricted. No hugging and no spiritual counseling, something I find extremely prejudicial. They do such a great job and should be credited with being a calming influence in a volatile place. My message for the church is about "overcoming evil with good," and I am collecting great stories, as examples.

Take five minutes now to pray for someone who may be annoying you. Pray for God's blessing on that person. Mentally, emotionally, financially, any area you can think of. Also, ask the Lord to help you look at them through His eyes, listen with His ears, and to have a mouth that speaks grace and life.

I'm learning a lot about the drug culture. A young woman told me that her suburb was just full of drug addicts. She could not avoid them, if she tried; so it's really hard for her to start over clean. I tried to guess the suburb. "Wrong," she said. It was quite a well-to-do area on the Bayside. I was shocked.

She went on to explain that there were two pharmacies, opposite each other, and *both* dispense methadone.

"So the druggies and the dealers are all over that street. You can't escape them, even to get a normal prescription filled."

I realized I probably wouldn't have recognised a druggie in *that* street, if I ran over one. *I would now.*

This woman explained the paradox of the "successful" drug users. The addiction means that when they need drugs, they become erratic. However, when they are on them, they calm down and can make sensible decisions.

One of her customers is a high profile, extremely wealthy business owner. The drugs make him feel powerful and confident. Ironically, when he is off them, he fears people suspect he *is* on them, because of his strange behaviour. How ironic!

The devil is such a deceiver. Fancy not only getting someone physically hooked; but having them believe their success is due to their drug taking. In the meantime, their lives are robbed.

I've since read a newspaper article describing the types of drugs different professions prefer. "Blue collar workers" prefer marijuana; whereas those in positions of higher "status," such as in the finance industry, prefer cocaine. Users claimed it kept them sharp under pressure. I'm not sure I'd like my investments looked after by someone on coke!

I've learned that there is a difference between a druggie and a junkie. I used the latter term and one of the girls "pulled me up," saying, "That's a really derogatory term. You are being insulting."

She then explained a junkie is the stereotypical "addict." They are the ones who have no remaining self-respect, and will do anything for a fix. They are often dirty, sick and broken. They are a small minority among drug addicts.

It's a widely held belief here, that "almost everyone uses drugs, even if it is just marijuana." Our unit is already over-crowded. Half the cells have a mattress on the floor; for a second occupant that the cell was not designed for. With the new random drug testing of drivers, we are expecting to be overflowing in here, before too long.

On a lighter note, these same girls are a lot of fun. They can be a bit edgy, if their methadone is delivered late; but other than that, they are perfectly normal. Well, perhaps *not*, because they love my singing!

We had a pleasant day, because the "Buy-ups" were delivered. This is where we receive our orders of personal items, coffee and tobacco for those who smoke.

After dinner one day I offered to sing a song. I did my best impression of singing "Dream a Little Dream." They all said "Wow you are so good!" I *can* carry a tune so the "bar" is not set very high!

The trick is to sing where the acoustics are most flattering. I won't be auditioning as a psalmist any time soon. Don't worry Becky and Aaron (Citipointe Church music leaders). Don't worry "Australian Idol!"

Amanda has been transferred to Helena Jones Centre, so I will probably go on Tuesday. *We had been told we would probably go at the same time.*

Jane, a strong black girl, said the others were wondering how I was feeling after "my little mate" had left. I was touched that they cared, and said I was happy to spend a bit more time with them. Jane, who happens to be gay, gave me a big hug and little "peck" kiss on the head. We do that; it was girl thing, not a gay thing; just like we might do at church. It's nice.

I have developed a great affection for these women. It's hard to imagine why they are in here. Most are drug related; they commit fraud to get money for drugs. They deal drugs to be able to pay for drugs. Some sell their bodies to get drugs. They do a "break-and-enter" to finance drugs. They assault people when on drugs.

A challenge my drug-addict friend faces is what to do, when she quits. "So much of your day is getting your fix. The rest of the day is getting money for the next fix. It's hard to know what to do when your whole life, and those of your associates, revolves around those goals."

How does a person keep occupied? They are not strong or reliable enough to work at a real job yet. Can they knit into a church? Theoretically, yes. However, leaders must be vigilant as the recovering drug addict needs supervision. Temptation is great, even after they are "clean."

Many of those on the "methadone program" still shoot up heroin. I'm told they have to shoot more, in order to be able to feel it. It's certainly not my area of expertise. Most of them started by trying to find something that would give them a lift out of their sadness and anger, usually rooted in abuse.

If so many women have been abused as children, there must be many more paedophiles than we think. Are there really such a small minority? If not a paedophile, then it was usually a predatory teenager.

One forty-year-old woman told me she was only twelve, when her fifteen-year-old cousin bullied her into having sex with him. He threatened to tell everyone they had done it anyway. Then, as she became a teenager in her small town, date rape was the normal culture of the youth. I know the town; there is a vibrant Christian Outreach Centre church there, thank God.

What is really going on in *your* town? Who can a twelve-year-old go to? Who will tell her that the local boys are not entitled to use her? Who will tell the *boys*? What are the parents teaching their kids about morals, or are they too busy both working, to have those conversations?

We must continue to fight the subcultures destroying our children right under our noses!

There are other women here for less dramatic reasons. They have done any one of the many things we might have done; and not got caught for. Sometimes they accumulated too many demerit points, and got booked, one-too-many times. Perhaps they had a car accident and someone was hurt. The same accident, the same misjudgment *without a person getting hurt* would have resulted in no jail time.

How many times have you changed a radio station or fiddled with something, while driving, and drifted across the line, then suddenly pulled back; relieved no one was there? It can happen to anyone.

Some women drove when their registration had run out. They could not pay the registration but still had transport needs. How does a person with a suspended licence, get her children to school or apply for a job? What if she doesn't live near public transport? In many areas you need a car to get to the public transport!

These are not lawless, rebellious teens.

Perhaps the answer is to restrict their driving to the "school run" and the job search. Not everyone is given permission to drive to work. One young woman was banned from driving for ten years.

Ten years! That was five years ago. She has missed out on jobs and is reluctant to start a family until she is free to drive.

She will be thirty-four by then.

That's enough seriousness. This morning I was summoned to the Health Centre. I didn't know why. When I got there the receptionist looked for my name on a list. "There I am!" I spotted it. Alas! I also spotted the title of the list: Mental Health.

My blood ran cold. 'I've done it now,' I thought. 'Someone has told on me for praying and now they think I'm crazy!' I tried to be calm, and act normal, as visions from *"One Flew over the*

Cuckoo's Nest" and *"Francis,"* tormented me. Fortunately, the appointment was just to check to see how I was coping. Apparently another box needed ticking. What a relief!

How can an institution address mental health, when it creates an environment that damages mental health? "Are you likely to self-harm? No. Box ticked! Nothing further required."

My appointment was to establish whether I was likely to self-harm, in which case I would be put into a cell with a camera, and made to take stupefying drugs. I had no false expectation that they actually cared about my mental well-being, so I gave the answers required, in order to be left alone.

They've messed with enough of my life without messing with the inside of my head too; that's my private space. As the German song goes, "Die Gedanken Sind Frei – My Thoughts are Free."

By the way, if you don't hear from me for a while, I might have been carted off to S4 with the criminally insane. No pens or paper there. No underwear is allowed, nothing that can be used for self-harm. It seems to me, if you weren't crazy when you got there, you would be by the time they let you out.

It's so boring here during the day, I decided to try to put on a concert. I have found three other girls willing to sing a song each, so we'll do that tomorrow afternoon. I'll let you know how it goes.

Live your faith like you really do believe it.

Love, Trish

New day, 6th letter, continued

21st February (Saturday)

Dear family and friends.

Bliss. Peace. Contentment. That is what I feel as I write. I am sure it is partly due to your prayers, partly to what the Lord is doing in my unit of twenty-something women, and partly due to what the Lord is doing in my own heart.

I no longer view them as horrid ninth graders! I have gotten to know many of them, cried with them, prayed for and encouraged them, and they me. Some of them are really, really funny. The language is decidedly "blue" but they don't notice and I prayed it would be like "white noise," so I barely notice it either. There only seem to be two words they use, neither of which refer to Jesus, which is a relief.

They do pretend to be shocked, when I come out with an observation or two. They have this idea that Christians are straight-laced Puritans who refuse to have fun. Of course, fun without drugs is an unusual concept for some of them. I have made great friends with some of the lesbians. They were teasing me about my love for the women here, and asking if I would "turn?"

I answered with a straight face, "Well, you never know, if it gets cold enough... but seriously, I love you in a *'healthy'* way."

Peals of laughter erupted at my use of the word "Healthy."

I did have an upset that made me livid.

I was running thirty laps of the basketball court (a touch over 2km or 1.2 miles), plus doing sit-ups. I am getting fitter and healthier. We can't go every day but I go whenever they let us. Loud music is always played while we work out.

I stopped to shoot some baskets and noticed the words of the song. I heard the F-word, again and again. I thought, 'this is wrong'. Should I complain? Maybe not, it's a risk that could backfire.

Then I made out the words, "Run, nigger, run!" being repeated in the song. That did it!

Never one to back away from looking foolish; I tapped on the supervisor's door. Her office overlooks the court.

"Um, excuse me; are you aware of the four letter words in the song being played?" She looked at me and asked, "Are you religious?" I hate religious stereotyping, so I avoided a direct answer.

"It's nothing to do with religion, I just didn't think the prison would condone offensive language in music it provides, it's insulting and disrespectful to the ladies, and *that* will hinder their rehabilitation, especially when there is a rule about us having to be polite."

She looked at me like I was from another planet and, just in case I had forgotten she reminded me "This is prison. That language is everywhere."

Not being one to easily take a hint, I pressed on.

"Yes, I am aware that even the guards use that language, but it can't be healthy for us. Besides, it's got racist words in it. The black girls would hate it!"

She put her pen down. "It's the women who choose the music. They write out a list and every six months I go out and buy it. If you don't like it you have two choices:

1) Don't come to gym, or

2) Write to the Director General."

"Well, it wouldn't be fair for me to miss out on exercise, and if the women have chosen it I won't complain. But tell me, do you have "Mama Mia?"

"NO!"

"Okay, thanks..."

At least I gave her a story to tell in the staff lunch room. When I told the girls back in the unit, instead of sharing my indignation, they laughed their heads off.

"Only you would care about that stuff, Trish!"

At a later date, I quietly asked my Aboriginal friends about it. They do hate it. It is racist; but they don't make waves.

I went to an Anglican service. I'll go to whatever is on offer. It was funny to hear some of the women chatting, on the way over, about how God had been "#%&*ing touching my life. There's nothing #%&*ing like God. He's #%&*ing great, man!" Right.

Oh, do you remember when I moaned about my hair, my sunburn, and a broken fly, and that all I needed was for a bird to poop on me? Well, even *that* finally happened in the yard the other day.

Our yard is completely caged and we have finches and parrots that sit on the top. *Yep*, I looked down, and there it was on my arm. The girls assure me it's good luck...

Luck? MY luck turns into funny, awkward, or embarrassing stories. At least they make me laugh.

For example: All our clothes, with the exception of underwear, are put in laundry bags to be washed downstairs. Consequently, I hand wash my knickers in the shower.

A few feet away from the shower is the toilet with its built-in hand basin in the top. At the rear of the hand basin are two buttons. Pressing one will flush the toilet, and the other activates a little bubbler for drinking water and hand washing.

The flushing is fierce, like that on an aeroplane, very loud. Sometimes, I would lean over the commode, and press for a drink; only to give myself a fright, as the toilet flushed with a loud suck!

Well, the simplest thing to do is wash my knickers in the shower, wring them out, and then reach across to pop them on the edge of the sink, ready to be hung up after I was dry.

Imagine my horror when I realised I had put my "undies" too close to the edge?

Plop! They dropped right into the commode! Eew! Reminding myself that it was only water, I fished them out, and gave them an extra thorough cleaning. I had no interest in sticking to the "three-minute shower limit" that night!

I'm sure there's a message in there, somewhere, for all of us. God just hasn't revealed it to me yet...

I read two daily devotionals in my Morning Prayer time:

1. "Every day with Jesus," and
2. "The Word for Today."

It's wonderful how the messages can be practically relevant on a given day. The recent theme of caring for others was very helpful; especially the one about knowing when to pull back.

Caring too much is what distorted my judgment and got me in here. Trying to fix one problem only created another. A professional would not have let emotions cloud their decision making.

I watch the Storm Financial situation unfolding on the news each day. It looks like someone will eventually go to jail; but who knows? It looks like there were inconsistencies at every point of some of those transactions. It will be difficult to apportion blame accurately.

Even in here I am asked to explain how the markets work, how to buy property, how investment loans work and other financial matters. I reluctantly explain the relationship between the value of the dollar and oil prices, the effect of the demand for coal, and why our economy relies so heavily on it.

My best financial advice to the girls in here is, "Stop dealing drugs, do a course, get to know God, and find a good church." God will unfold His plan for your life; trust Him!

There are really only two rules for investing.

Rule Number One: "Never invest more than you can afford to lose!"

Rule Number Two: "See Rule One!"

If you find your investment goes into liquidation, I can promise you, investors will receive nothing. Anything realised will go to paying the liquidation company. You might as well write it off and get over it, quickly.

Refer to Rule Number One again.

My business advice did not go unchallenged.

One "businesswoman" had made a lot (thousands), in just three days. It enabled her to buy a new car for cash. She couldn't really see why closing her drug dealing business was a good idea. She has no work experience and no other skills. I did point out that she was obviously good at sales and marketing!

She also said she had to "deal" to make the money required, to keep paying her lawyer. *Hmm*, I'm sure some lawyers have a "don't ask, don't tell" policy to ensure they keep getting paid.

I had to concede that argument, as her logic was better than mine...

I still discouraged illegal activities, of course!

Same Letter, Same Day

Saturday evening:

We had a concert this afternoon which was a huge success! I was "M.C." (emcee/Master of Ceremonies) and able to get everybody gathered to listen and join in. A wild looking Aboriginal lady sang beautifully, some women who had been too scared were coaxed up, and I sang a couple of songs as well.

Audiences don't get much tougher than that one! We had a ball.

One woman who *had* been "hearing voices" telling her to cut herself, said she felt "set free" by the joyfulness around her.

I performed "Miss Celie's Blues" from *"The Color Purple,"* and they loved it, especially the dark girls. It's a song from one woman to another about staying strong.

I used a towel as a feather boa and really hammed it up! I expected a few sneers and accusations of being a show off, (which I am, of course), but there were none. Even the officers enjoyed it. That was a relief because we are actually not allowed to have "unauthorised gatherings!"

I suspect if I had sung the earlier mentioned sixteenth century folk song "Die Gedanken Sind Frei – My Thoughts are Free," we would have been shut down. I'd be carted off for inciting rebellion... a line of that song is, "And should tyrants taken me and throw me in prison, my thoughts will burst freely like blossom in season..."

A big "Thank You" goes to those who have written to me. It always gives me a lift and helps me feel like I am still connected. I am able to ring my family most days. I miss them terribly. The days feel very slow, so I pray for the time to feel like it passes quickly. That prayer has not been answered yet. A day feels like a week. A week feels like a month.

1 month down, seven to go. I try not to think about it. I am praying that my daughters will not develop any long-terms "hang-ups" from this journey we are going through as a family.

I am especially grateful to Pastor Luke Harris and the "Citikidz" team, for supporting Justin, Chelsea, Felicity and Olivia at church. Our parents and our Pastors Mark and Leigh Ramsey have been wonderful, too.

Take care of each other.

God Bless,

Trish

P.S. (The following letter was written by Justin when he typed out my letter as an email on March 3rd. It takes more than the usual time for letters to reach loved ones, because they are read and monitored by prison officials, before being sent on.)

I spoke to Trish on the phone this morning; she had "hit the wall". This is the first time she has cried since being sentenced. She was trying to find out when she was being moved to Helena Jones (promised three weeks now) and was pretty much "fobbed off." She was told by management they were waiting for a psychologist's report. When she made enquiries, a psychologist told her that was rubbish, and such a report wasn't needed for her to go to Helena Jones house.

Please pray for the management.

Even on this call to Trish she said if God wants her to stay where she is, then fine.

Thanks for your prayers.

Justin

7th Letter

22nd February

Hello Friends,

Every now and then, something happens to remind me why the nurse delivers medication to the unit three times a day. I must be vigilant as a normal conversation can result in great offence. I believe an unsettling influence entered with a particular girl, Sam.

Sam arrived last week, and, very quickly, said the "Sinner's prayer" with Sandra. I found it hard to warm to her, and just being polite required self-discipline. I figured it might be a "spirit of rejection" in *her* trying to make me reject her, so I tried to help her with the concepts of God, and how to handle conflict with prayer.

Over a period of a few days, more girls complained of her pushiness and laziness, as she repeatedly asked for things and for her meals to be got for her, while she was on the phone or doing something else.

I stay out of the politics for obvious reasons. However, when she asked me to move seats so that *she* didn't have to sit next to someone at our table, I thought, 'Enough is enough.'

I said, "No. I won't help you bear a grudge."

Sam announced she had "astral travelled" last night, and when I probed further, she said she had been involved in "Wicca," a type of witchcraft and the occult.

The gauntlet was thrown down, but I did not immediately respond. Instead, I resumed my prayer walk through the unit, quietly taking authority. In the meantime, several "little but serious" conflicts were erupting. I challenged Sam about praying for God's blessing on those upsetting her; and, even though she said she had, I could tell she was lying. She walked away very quickly, seeking sympathy elsewhere.

I also let her know people were saying she needed to do more for herself. She became upset and angry. I guess I still don't know when to shut up. I am getting better though. I am not intimidated.

Sandra and I believe there is a "Jezebel spirit" operating. Jezebel was the wife of an ancient King who tried to murder the prophet of God. She was manipulative and cunning. We refer to a Jezebel spirit as the quiet force behind someone who appears normal; but is deliberately causing trouble *behind the scenes* to undermine people. Rather than be open about their trouble-making, they manipulate others into causing trouble. It could be because they are jealous, needing power, they love stirring up strife or are just plain nasty.

The key for me is maintaining my love for someone I think may be playing disruptive games. It's also tempting to confront; but doing so usually backfires.

As I pray, I believe the strategy is to keep taking authority over the atmosphere, and "praying for the blood of Jesus to cover everyone," because we don't wrestle with people; but spiritual influences. In Christian culture, the blood of Christ is what washes our sins away. The blood defeated Satan, at Calvary, and is a key in spiritual warfare. There is power in that blood. That is why Holy Communion is honoured in every Christian denomination. It is a symbol of victory over evil.

All the women believe I am "nice," but some of them are beginning to see that I am not a push-over. I will exhort them to higher standards.

One beautiful Aboriginal lady had been coerced into making a false accusation about someone else. She felt bad about it. I was able minister to her, and encouraged her not to be intimated. She then went and apologised to the *wronged* person. While ministering to her, I spoke about the gifts the Lord has placed in her life. I believe she will speak, and minister to women and also to Indigenous children; *if she stays out of trouble and maybe, even if she doesn't!* I encouraged her to find a good church that is spirit-filled, when she gets out. Maybe she will and maybe she won't.

Some days are smooth, and some filled with these "issues." It's easy to forget how touchy my fellow prisoners can be. Because of the combination of mental illness, demonic influence, and plain bitchiness, one can never be sure what will set someone off.

I am not afraid, nor should you be for me. However, even though "Blessed are the peacemakers," *that blessing* is likely to be linked to the "blessing" we get by "copping flack" for doing what we believe is right! Does that make sense?

Hopping in to make peace can often cause more problems, so my strategy is to, instead, spend the next day quietly minding my own business, but using what I call "targeted prayer."

On a lighter note, the black girl in charge of the kitchen has almost never spoken to me. I've been working on her. She is quite funny and rarely refers to anything without giving it a particularly "blue" adjective as a prefix such as "Give me the #%&* broom." Sometimes a noun is simply replaced with "blue" noun as in "Give me the #%&*."

Not that I find swearing funny; but she is a baby faced Aborigine in a rich shade of brown. She has big, brown, deep set eyes, a bright pink tongue and a very quick wit. She is so cute; sometimes it's hard not to laugh at what she comes out with.

Today she decided to offer me a piece of "Caramel Slice," she'd made by microwaving a tube of condensed milk. She even called me "Sista-girl," a title she normally reserves to her Indigenous and close friends.

The concert yesterday had obviously given me some kudos in the unit. I'll be able to trade on that for a while anyway.

7th Letter, continued

23rd February

I have been informed I will be going to Helena Jones when my psych report is checked off.

A seventeen-year-old arrived today. How does a seventeen-year-old land here? Drugs. She has been in foster care all her life and went off the rails at fourteen. I had a few quiet words with her; but who knows? Several older women have tried to talk sense into her.

Nobody here likes to see really young ones come in. She says she will give up the drugs. Her friend is here and does heroin. The friend has no intention of quitting, she says she loves it.

One of the moral dilemmas or hypocrisies of prison life is illustrated by the seventeen-year-old being allowed to purchase tobacco.

It is illegal to supply tobacco to a person under the age of eighteen; but a prison is doing it. More to the point, we are relieved that they let her.

It would cause all sorts of problems if a drug addict cannot at least smoke cigarettes; it would also create more problems for other prisoners who have to live with one! Will the system offer "relaxation training" as a substitute? Imagine the media reaction to that! "Crims to enjoy stress relief classes!"

Sometimes, the women talk in fear about another prison being built out at Gatton, several hours west of Brisbane. It is reported to be a Maxi-prison that will bring industry and employment to the area.

The only catch is that it will be a NO SMOKING facility! I'm not sure why, or if it's even true; but such a rule will probably do more to deter crime than anything else!!!

If it is for politically correct or health reasons then one would expect it to be non-smoking for the staff as well. Good luck to the recruitment agency!

I wonder how the various staff members end up here. No one dreams of becoming a corrections officer!

I am a terrible "sticky-beak." The women here are fascinating. I can't help asking questions about their scars, veins, their history, and what makes them choose the drugs they do. Fortunately they indulge me. They think I'm a bit odd; but harmless and nice.

They accept me being "overly religious" because I care about them. They are happy to educate me. Sometimes I surprise them because they can have wrong assumptions about Christians. For example, Karen is a gentle soul who had been pack-raped on her first date. It happened to all her friends, so she thought it was "just what young ones do," in her town. She is in for breaching her parole by shop-lifting. She can't help stealing and is actually banned from her local shopping centre. Christians were a strange lot to her. I made a joke and Karen exclaimed, "Trish, I am disgraced at you!"

Her phrase was funnier than my joke. So sweet.

Well, Sam, the woman who snapped at me yesterday after I told her I wasn't going to help her bear a grudge, just apologised; so I made her promise to be nicer to someone she had been tormenting. I had to press home my advantage, while I had it. She asked me to let the others know of her apology as they had given her a hard time over it.

Forgiveness is a touchy subject in here. Loving your enemies is a hard sell in church, let alone in here. The lovely thing to see is how quickly the Holy Spirit moves when one of the women does pray for her "enemy."

God is being so good. Can I suggest an exercise this week where you pick someone who bugs you, and you say *nothing* but target them in prayer? I would love to hear the results!

7th Letter, continued

25th February

Today I am thirty-nine. Tomorrow I am forty! I can't believe I'm spending my fortieth birthday in prison. Yuck!

Until recently, I felt reluctant to turn forty at all. Then I planned to do something extraordinary, like when I went Bungy Jumping the year I turned twenty-one.

I had visions of a tandem sky-dive. Turning forty in prison did not seem quite as thrilling. I wanted to ignore it.

However, I have come to see the enormous blessing in being here. I placed my "buy up" order on Sunday and delivery is tomorrow. I ordered a "generic" fruit cake (the only kind we can buy), to share with the women just in case I had not been moved to Helena Jones. I praised God for the "admin" delay because I'd prefer to be with the people I know and have come to love.

One girl who had been quite mixed up and is very tough is going to court tomorrow. She asked me to pray for her, which I did. *Someone else told me she was facing murder charges.*

Late this afternoon another girl, Belle, from the "in" crowd was on the phone. (Yes, even prison has an "in" crowd.) I wasn't listening, but I heard the word "Ephesians" and had to look up. She caught my eye and grinned. After hanging up, she came over to me as I sat against the besser block wall in the concrete yard, and announced, "I did the 'born again' thing the first time I came to jail when I was seventeen!" She has been in and out of jail ever since. She is now twenty-six. Between drugs and prostitution, she has quite a history.

Belle now had a fiancé who asked her to read Ephesians, apparently he is a Christian. I shared with her for a bit and she asked me to write out some prayers. We prayed, holding hands but with our eyes open and not looking at each other, so as not to draw attention. My heart just melted. She has a delightful personality, big blue "Bette Davis" eyes, and tight curly golden hair that had been long until two other jealous prostitutes beat her up and cut it all off.

I prayed that the Holy Spirit would fill her. I bound rebellion, addiction and lust. I also spoke of her value to the Lord and how much she is loved. I kissed her lovely, "dolly-like" head. When she turned to me, she had tears pouring down. Around us, women were smiling and nodding encouragingly. We hadn't fooled anyone! Then I laughed and said "Oh heavens! If you cry I'll be in trouble. It'll be off to the D.U. (Detention Unit) with Jenkins!" I joked.

There is nothing so fulfilling as ministering to a precious life. Belle is a popular girl and the women could tell she was blessed by what happened. There was a warm feeling of "community" all around.

Then a softly-spoken, full-blooded Aboriginal lady told me she had a birthday present for me, and she didn't want to wait till tomorrow. She took me to her cell door and instructed me to close my eyes; a few seconds later, she said, "Now smell". A lovely, floral fragrance wafted up. She was giving me a bottle of aromatherapy shampoo and a pretty face washer. I was touched and she was beaming.

This is a lady who had given me a page she had coloured beautifully with pencils, as a gift for me to post to my little girls. They in turn drew pictures for her, which my husband posted in. She was "tickled pink!"

To top off my happy anticipation, Mum was finally able to book a visit for tomorrow! It has been five weeks! What a great birthday present. There will be "buy up" arriving, a cake with the girls, and a visit from mum. Who could ask for more? *Did I really say that?*

Even though I will not be with my family, the Lord has shown me how effective I am being here and that gives me great joy. I feel sad for Justin, the girls, and my family not being able to celebrate with me, but we will party when I am home again.

7th Letter, continued

28th February

Well, my special day was everything I expected. Even better; in that it was a happy day for everyone in the unit. After dinner, I stood on the bottom stair in the hall and sang, "Bridge over Troubled Waters."

I told my beautiful, dysfunctional audience that the song reflected how I felt about them.

I still need to take charge of the atmosphere in prayer, daily, as all sorts of influences arrive with the new comers; and as current ladies' past issues are provoked. The tone of the unit changes as the population turns over.

My flesh rose up yesterday as a young woman, who giggles about doing drugs, went to use the phone before me. I thought she had tried to skip the line and I let her know my irritation. Today, I found her and apologised. I was rude, and I didn't give her a chance to explain. She had left the line briefly, to go inside, and no one was left to vouch for her place.

It may sound petty; but the phone use is a precious thing here. We only get ten minutes at a time, and there are usually around twenty-five of us in the unit, trying to use one phone.

I have one beautiful friend who is slowly coming to see that Christ is real. She is reading the testimony of a lady who went to prison, and found Christ. It includes how the author got filled with the Spirit.

This particular woman was not molested, had been in a nice marriage with a good man; but had always felt gay.

How do we, as a church, respond to these women?

We love them the same as we love anybody else who comes in the door. It's God's *kindness* that leads to repentance, not judgment. If Christ has drawn them, He will minister to them, and set them free, without condemnation.

Same as the rest of us.

In 2008, a well-respected prophet said that I would "have a message that won't be popular with everyone." *Great, as if I haven't caused enough controversy already!*

Oh, well, His will be done.

Love you Church,

Trish

Journal notes

Well, any chance of appeal has been stuffed by the incompetence of the system, and I'm not sure who is responsible. I received a summary of the court proceedings from my lawyer, telling me I must lodge an appeal against the sentence, by February 21.

The letter was dated February 9; but the envelope was stamped as "Received 24th February at the prison mail processing centre."

I didn't receive it until *after* that date.

When I asked my lawyer about it, he said "A successful appeal would only reduce my sentence by a month or two, which is hardly worth it."

A month or two! Easy for him to say!

I can't bear to read the details of the document again. It just details that "the worst thing that can happen" is really happening to me! As far as the world is concerned, I am officially, a *bad* person, and not worth fighting for any longer.

God, you must have a plan for this length of time.

Help me see it.

8th Letter

1st March

We had a surprisingly good chapel service this morning. It was the Uniting Church's turn. I wasn't going to go, because I thought it would be boring. How shallow is that? Plus, I wanted to go running again.

Sandra reminded me that we needed to be an example. She was right, of course, so off we went. There was quite a large crowd as the officer on duty did not dispute the rule on numbers for church.

An old lady ministered. She played a Pat Morgan song that I remembered from years ago, "Never Give Up." The Presence of God fell in the room and, once again, I was asked to pray and explain the Holy Spirit.

Great!

Would I get slammed for it again?

I decided reverse psychology was the softest approach, and began with, "I am not allowed to lay hands on you, because God might show up like last time…"

"Tell us more!" They called out. They knew very well that someone had fallen down, under the power of God. Perhaps that is why there were more attendees this time. Everyone likes a drama. So I told them what I was not allowed to talk about and why. I told them I was not allowed to pray out loud; but they could approach me privately back in the unit.

In effect, I taught, without appearing to teach.

I knew they would respond. I had women from other units ask me to pray for them, after the service.

Sandra, on the other hand, has not been forbidden. She preached and prayed with gusto. She even prophesied over two women. A few ladies gave testimonies.

Sandra is "called" to preach. What a testimony! She was forced into prostitution at the age of eleven, by *her own parents*. This wasn't India, it was Brisbane. She ended up living on the streets, had bad relationships, had her children taken from her by Family Services, and has been in and out of jail.

Then she gave her heart to the Lord. Gradually, she has gained a sound mind, become alcohol and drug free, and has even given up smoking and sugar. Many addicts are heavy-handed, when it comes to sugar. Sandra is leading people to Jesus and unofficially "pastors" them. She is an inspiration.

Sandra suffers mockery and persecution from other prisoners. Some feel entitled to look down on people who have been prostitutes. I don't understand that myself. I guess it makes people feel less crappy about themselves if they perceive someone else as "lower" than them.

I expected the women who had suffered abuse, to have understanding and compassion on others. It's rare. That need to feel superior to someone is rooted in insecurity, and occurs in all areas of society; but especially here, where fear and mistrust make self-preservation the priority.

There are a number of women here I assumed were ten years older than me. In fact, they are considerably younger than me; but wrong choices, and a rough life, has aged them. Their faces and bodies have been ravaged. They try to talk sense into the youngest girls, who don't realise how brief the window of opportunity is to create a good life. The young ones can't imagine becoming like these older ones; they don't seem to care about the effects of their lifestyle or their jail time. They live in the moment; not caring about the social problems they contribute to.

Speaking of social problems, it's one thing to campaign against abortion, but how will you assist a dysfunctional young woman with raising her baby, especially if she hasn't learned how to *live* herself? It's hard. It's costly. It's time-consuming. It often creates *more* problems to deal with. Yet, building a better society is what we do.

It's important that we are not too busy doing God's work that we don't see God's child in front of us. It's important to help those in Third World countries, but we must not forget the poor among us. "Poor" is not always financial, either.

When someone accepts Christ, I encourage them to seek out a Bible believing church. I really hope I am doing the right thing. Once, I had blind faith in our kind of church's acceptance and willingness to help the broken to get back on track. Unfortunately, not all churches are as accepting as Jesus. It's OK to have a style, an appeal to a particular demographic, but not to the extent that a person feels unwelcome, unworthy, or intimidated.

Church, we must be mindful to treat those who can add no perceived "value" to our programs; with the same honour given to our best talents and our biggest givers. Beware that, as you seek wealth creation to fund noble programs, the wealth creation does not become more important, than the people the program is intended for.

Let your love extend beyond your church. I worked with a lady once who was so negative, critical and sour, that I wanted to avoid her. Her expression of disapproval had created a permanently wrinkled nose, and a pursed mouth like a cat's rear. I attempted to share the love of Christ with her; but she rebuffed me defensively, and assured me she was an active member of a Charismatic church!

I wanted to suggest she didn't tell anyone else...

Please let Bronwen Healy know her book, *"Trophy of Grace,"* is very popular here. She is well-respected among the women. She may not remember who I am, but I went along to help her bless the street women, mostly prostitutes, in The Valley, one Valentine's Day evening.

A group of us spent that night giving those women a manicure, massage, facial, foot massage and other things to make them feel good about themselves. It was a very special time.

We can change our society for the better. This "underclass" of people might be difficult, and they might be at the bottom, but they still matter. Will you love the broken and hurting, the violent, the morally bankrupt, and the angry?

They are not easy to be around, but they need you.

> "That which you do to the least of these...you do to me...."

> Matthew 25 *again*

The following won't sound very holy but it was very funny. A few of the girls had giggled in church and mocked the participants. *The officer did nothing to discourage them which disappointed, but didn't surprise me.*

When we exited the building, a tall black lady turned on these girls, and said,

"You #$%&*ing #$&*s! You were so #$%&*ing disrespectful you #$&*s. IF you #%&*ing talk and laugh next time I'll #%&*ing tear you a-$%&*ing-part! Do you #%&*ing #%&*s hear me? This is CHURCH! Have some #%&*ing respect!"

Oh my! Gotta love that passion for Jesus!

8th Letter, continued

3rd March

Four ladies gave their hearts to the Lord over the weekend. Then, at the gym, I was approached by a fifth lady asking for prayer. I didn't know her; she was from another unit, but she had heard me speak at chapel, in the past. I led her to the Lord. It always touches me to see the light in people's faces, when they *really* encounter the Holy Spirit.

Ironically, the officer this week had only let seven people go. I gave my place to someone else, so they could go, and this girl had been looking for me. Getting conflicting instructions from officers is not unusual. Inefficiency and inconsistency is entrenched in the protocols here.

Suggestions from prisoners are usually dismissed out of hand. They certainly don't like us reminding them of how the rules are normally applied. I don't know if it's due to the assumption we are stupid or that it would be "unseemly" for them to heed people like us.

I had a bit of a "melt-down" this morning. My day went as follows:

A few days ago I got a new cell-mate; due to over-crowding. I'd had several sleepless nights due to her constant snoring. Sometimes, she actually stops breathing for long seconds, so I would shake her to change her breathing pattern. Some nights are worse than others, and this was a bad one.

Doesn't sleep apnoea require surgery? I don't know how dangerous it is. I woke her, and propped her up more. She suffers cramps due to coming off heroin so some evenings I massage her calves to give her some relief. She is younger than me, but has become more like a big sister, because she is so street-wise.

I sleep on the floor, because she's a big girl, and it's too awkward for her get up off the floor. Our pillows and mattresses are waterproof, so they crackle with each movement.

In the morning, I told the nurse about my concerns for my cell-mate's breathing.

"Well, she'll have to report it herself. It's got nothing to do with you."

"She can't report what she is not aware of."

"It's none of your business."

"What if something happens to her?"

"I've told you, it's up to her to report it. Next!"

So much for the "duty of care" they go on about. If it doesn't have a "box" that can be "ticked" then it doesn't fit; so, it doesn't exist.

I had just started to talk to Justin on the phone, when "Activities" was announced. I had to hang up abruptly and rush inside as only seven are allowed to go. I wasn't quick enough and missed out, so no running for me today.

The Sentence Management fellow turned up. I waited my turn in order to ask him again when I was going to Helena Jones Centre. He asked if I had organised my psychology clearance report. The first time I had asked him about my transfer, he didn't mention it. I had not been aware that I was supposed to have one. So, I had asked at the medical centre about it, with some confusing results.

I told him, "Yes, I followed it up, and they told me it was unnecessary for me to have their department's approval. They said your office contacted them and was told I'm all clear to go!"

"Well, I need it in writing. Next!"

"I'm sure your office would already have it."

"Next!"

"But..."

"Next!"

Amanda has already gone to Helena Jones. I still have no idea when I'm going. We stay here until Sentence Management classifies us. I've been classified as "non-violent, low risk." Therefore, I am on a list waiting to go to Helena Jones Centre. It's on busy, Sandgate Road in the city, at Albion.

I'd used that road many times, worked in the area, and had *never* noticed the place. I wonder how many locals know what it is and who lives there?

I got my head bitten off, for looking at an open book on a table. Someone else had been reading it. Then one of the "Alpha females," who I usually got on with, accused me of *thinking* she had a demon. Well, she probably does, but I didn't pursue an argument.

It's hard to be surrounded by people who are medicated for mental issues. It's ironic how *over-sensitive* "tough" people can be. I imagine it's even harder, when they are not medicated! This girl is awaiting trial for murder.

I was finally able to ring Justin back. It was all a bit much and I cried. I hung up, went to the end of the cage and, finally had a cry for me. They were the first tears of self-pity I'd shed, since before I was sentenced.

Suddenly, I was surrounded by women comforting me. Even the "Alpha female" was remorseful; I was touched by that. Most girls are afraid of her; but I am not. Perhaps that is why we get along? It's strange that I fear no one.

So it was a challenging day. I am grateful for your prayers, as it is easy to get discouraged here. It's hard to accept I am really in prison. I get notices from the prison referring to "Prisoner Jenkins," and I think, *"Who is she?"*

8th Letter, continued

5th March

It's not yet 7 a.m. Thursday morning. I've been seeking the Lord on my face. While I appreciate your prayers for my safety and wellbeing, I am more interested in being effective.

Please pray that the Lord does what he needs to do *in* me, so I don't get in the way of what he wants to do *through* me.

I may, or may not, go to the half-way house today. It's a better place to be, yet I don't want to leave here, until my work is done. There are a few women I am targeting in prayer. Perhaps it is a case of "the poor you will always have with you."

In other words, there will be more hurt criminals coming through, no matter when I leave. I hate to leave these girls. Sandra is doing a great job, but she too, needs encouragement.

It's odd to feel reluctant to leave prison. It's not because I have become comfortable; I dealt with self–indulgence last week. My fear is that I have not maximised my effectiveness. That's not to say I'm being pushy; I need to be more sensitive to the leading of the Spirit.

I am trying to remember what Ps Clark Taylor taught us years ago. He emphasised "settling into Jesus," practicing "Words of Knowledge," giving words of wisdom and healing, but most of all, showing His Love and Kindness. It's God's *kindness* that leads to repentance (Romans 2:4).

I am surrendered to His will and devoted to these daughters of the living God. Please pray for me to be effective in His hands.

Love from your sister,

Trish

Journal notes

Almost everyone but me is tattooed. Some of the artwork is quite elaborate. Some of it is awful. Some people like to create a tattoo as a "memento" of their stay here. I find tracing pictures and drawing *on paper* quite relaxing, and I do it in letters for my girls.

I ordered some glittery gel pens to make pretty pictures. One of the women asked to borrow my purple gel pen.

When I got it back, it was ruined; the ink was all smudged in the tube. I have to admit it was used to make a lovely picture – on someone's foot! Out in the yard, we huddled behind the clothes horse. If they had been caught, they would have both been put in the D.U.

I sat, fascinated, watching an artist at work. The sparkly purple ink had been squeezed into a teaspoon. An outline of a design had been drawn across her client's foot, above the toes. The artist had prepared her tool, a paperclip unwound and sharpened by rubbing the end on the concrete.

She dipped it into the magic fluid and then used it to puncture the skin of her client, carefully following the line of her drawing.

I was fascinated.

The artist turned her face away to cough. "I'm real careful," she said. "I don't want to get any of my 'Hep C' germs on your skin where I've pricked it."

That was thoughtful of her. She offered to give me a tattoo, but I politely declined. I'm not into tattoos and, I didn't want the free dose of Hepatitis C that might come with it!

I've heard the prison is rampant with drugs; but I haven't noticed any. I occasionally see women appear under the influence. One new girl walked around like a zombie with dark circles under her eyes. Someone said she would have found drugs hidden in the watch-house. I have no idea how.

"Remember how filthy the place was?"

"Yes."

"Well a "fit" can be hidden in that environment." A "fit" refers to the "gear" (utensils) required for drug consumption, such as a syringe.

"Oh, that's not exactly hygienic then," I said with distaste.

"I don't think she cares."

I later learned the girl had "banked" all sorts of things in a pill jar.

It sounds naïve, but I have no idea how drugs get in here. I'm aware that women can "bank" them; but once they are in here, how do they get more? I imagine it can only be through visitors or staff. Visitors could smuggle them in, and children are not allowed to be touched by officers, when they visit.

One visiting day, my parents had observed a sniffer dog, showing persistent interest in a toddler, during the visitor screening process. Even if a prisoner obtained them from the child, retrieving and getting drugs through the body search after a visit, would require some ingenuity. As for prison staff, I don't know their security procedures; but it wouldn't surprise me. There is a kind of "unclean" about some people, that doesn't refer to dirt. We should be kind to all, but extra careful around a few. "Be wise as serpents, and harmless as doves." Matt 10:16.

It would be difficult to work here and remain untainted. Some manage it; others are clearly affected by the negative influences around them. Perhaps I have just been spoilt by having dealt with mostly respectable people in my everyday life.

News of scandals doesn't seem to reach outside. We were all put in lockdown, while an ambulance came and took away the body of a lady, who died in the yard next to ours. The girls from that unit told us later, that the woman had been asleep, when the medication trolley arrived.

When the woman awoke, she asked the officers if she could have her medication; but they refused, saying she should have come when it was called. Later, in the yard, the woman had a fit and died at some point. I don't know if it was there, or later at hospital.

The officers rushed in and demanded to know who hit her. Everyone could attest that no one had. We could hear the commotion over the wall, but not the details. We were all then locked into our cells, while the ambulance came.

I wonder what they told the woman's family...

Thanks to another scandal, we are not allowed to use the toilet in the gym. Rumour has it that it's where an officer and a prisoner used to have sex. She got pregnant and was sent to a far-away prison. I don't know if he was sacked, or transferred, or how his wife took it...

Now, if we need to use the bathroom, we have to return to our unit, and are not allowed back for that session. *Yeah, that's the right response to inappropriate behaviour by an officer; punish the rest of the prisoners!*

Like I said before, it would be difficult to remain untainted by this place.

It's these things that make me wary of the official prison rhetoric. One thing I am not naïve about is human nature. A uniform does not make a person "good;" a criminal record does not make a person "bad."

More importantly, the lack of a criminal record does not mean a person is not a criminal already... perhaps they just haven't been caught yet.

Fortunately, some of the officers are decent folk, just doing their job, which only proves it is possible to remain "untainted."

It also means the environment is not an excuse for the officers who treat us disrespectfully.

9th Letter

Hello my friends,

I received a parcel of letters today. Among them were emailed messages you sent to Justin for me. He prints them out and pops them in an envelope, with his own letter, to me. I so appreciate hearing from friends. I'm especially touched to hear from people whom I have not personally met. *It amazed me that my letters went "viral," forwarded over the Internet; and strangers wrote to encourage me. They told of how my letters touched them!*

I prayed today for a lady who has a particular job. It's a hard job for her, and people often complain about it not being done right. I won't go into detail as I don't want her identified when the prison reads this letter.

Her job was doing laundry. We each had a bag we put our laundry in. Our bags have our cell numbers on them. We write a list of what is in our bag. She was supposed to put a bagful into the washing machine, then the dryer, then put it back into its numbered bag. If items, such as towels, were not quite dry, she could use the clothes horse in the yard which also doubled as a screen behind which tattoos were done. Unfortunately, things often went missing or got mixed up.

Anyway, her difficulties make her snappy and a few women were fed up. I could see trouble looming, so I got in first and asked her, "You know that thing I'm not allowed to talk about?"

"Yes" she answered.

"I'm not offering, but um, if you had something you wanted someone to pray for, I wouldn't say no. As long as you don't tell anyone and get me into trouble, of course."

"My kids," she answered, getting teary. I hadn't expected that. Once again, I marvelled at my own selfishness for not seeing beyond the surface issues (the ones that affect *me*). So I prayed

117

for her kids, and covered and bound everything else while I was at it; including repenting together of our attitudes. I also prayed for her to have a clear head, to do her job well...

The irritation in the unit simply dissolved.

Prayer is so much more effective, than advice. Imagine the conflicts we would avoid, if we applied that strategy all the time!

Officially, lesbian relationships are not allowed; but they are condoned. Women in relationships share cells. It doesn't bother me, except that it's unfair to those who don't have access to their male partners. There are no conjugal visits here. (Irk! Not exactly romantic!)

Occasionally, there is lewd behaviour in the yard. One time, without thinking, I instinctively called out, "Stop that!" They looked at me; one gave me a rude gesture and the other gave me a mouthful of language. The behaviour would have been just as offensive if they were "straight" people.

One could be forgiven for thinking lesbians are a protected species in here. Apparently, a chaplain had been banned for saying homosexuality is a sin. The women complained of discrimination, of course. I'm saddened at the lack of wisdom on the part of the chaplain.

These women have much more desperate needs for ministry than being criticised for taking comfort, in a miserable environment. Perhaps it bothered him more than it bothered the Lord?

I am more bothered if someone is nasty.

I don't expect non-Christians to act like Christians. Is someone living a de facto relationship any more "godly" than a homosexual? No. What I do know is, people either have a relationship with Jesus, or they don't. Knowing him, helps us make godly choices, more than other people's opinions.

Don't get me wrong, people need to be taught right and wrong. However, one "revelation" from the Lord is a more powerful catalyst for change, than the most sophisticated personal development program.

To be fair, most of the butch lesbian officers are very professional and polite. They don't talk down to us or play mind games. I'm glad they are good at their job, because they seem to represent a large proportion of the staff. Admittedly, it's disturbing at strip search time, after a visit; but, I just "close my eyes and think of England," as they say!

I have been showing different ones how to respond quickly to a setback. When we get bad news, it hurts, but how far that hurt travels into our heart, largely depends on how we think about it. I encourage the women to get hold of God as soon as possible, to pray blessings on the person who has hurt them, and praise God that he is in control.

God uses everything to draw people to himself, including, for example, an abusive parent causing trouble for his or her grown daughter's family. *I am fortunate to have caring parents helping Justin take care of our girls. Some women here have dysfunctional parents creating problems for their families, and the women are unable to do anything about it. It's frightening.*

Do you think it's hard for *you* to pray for someone who has offended you? Imagine growing up in a family where you are not shown love, nothing is forgiven, and everything is avenged, then being asked to pray a blessing on someone they think insulted them! That is what I was asking of some of these women. If they can do it; why not you?

I was able to chat with a particular chaplain, Donna. She has a wonderful gift of love. She is respected by the women and is a very effective minister. I would recommend her to speak to any churches about what her job is like. She can offer keys to helping people who may have been here or may be heading this way!

I had the privilege of praying for Donna. The words of knowledge and prophecy I had for her really touched her heart and provided answers she was seeking. The irony of a prisoner ministering to a chaplain was not lost on us!

Every societal group seems to have its "in" crowd. Here is no different. These girls are confident, tough and know each other well. One group has a ritual of making a hot chocolate, just before "lock down," in the evenings. My new cellmate is one of them. She must have told them I was OK, because I was actually invited to join them. The hot chocolate is expensive and has to be ordered specially on our "buy up" forms. To have someone offer to make me one, from their packet, was significant. I was touched and in an odd way, felt honoured.

Thank you to those who offered advice on certain types of people. It confirmed I am doing the right thing by just loving them and sharing Christ's Love. The Lord chooses when to work on areas of our lives. Isaiah 58 is very clear that he hates "the pointing of the finger" among us.

I would love to keep hearing from you, either by writing directly, or via email back to Justin.

Be blessed. Remember to keep the main thing as the main thing.

Trish Jenkins,

On Assignment.

Journal notes

A very scary, black girl, Vy, arrived. She joined our meal table and pointed out where she had scratched a pattern on it, during a previous visit, as a way of claiming the table. Everyone seemed afraid of her. I'm not stupid, so I stayed quiet.

As it turned out, there were advantages to having her at our table. It's common for sneaky people to steal other table's allotted margarine or sugar. Well, our margarine went missing and Vy went off! Her brand of language, her threats and persuasion were delivered so well, it was almost poetry! She finished her threat with "...and don't think I won't, 'cause I've done it before!"

The margarine magically reappeared.

Afterwards, I leaned toward her and quietly said, "I'm very glad you're on our table!" Up until then, she had ignored me, because she made it clear she hated white girls, but now she glanced at me, with a nod.

Sometime later, she mentioned she had been to Helena Jones before. I asked her what it was like.

"They're all dogs," she said. Unlike in the movies where the top convict is referred to as the "top dog," here a dog is a tattletale. It's the worst kind of insult.

I then asked her, "Have you got any advice for me?"

"Yeah, be a dog."

I was surprised. "I won't do that," I said.

She looked at me, "Yeah? You're going there 'cause you're a "stiff." You better be a dog, too, because that's what they do there."

"That's not me," I replied. She grinned. I couldn't believe she was recommending I play that game.

Someone else took me aside and said, "Don't go talking about the God stuff at Helena Jones. We like it here, but they won't; just be quiet."

Vy turned out to be right about the tattle-tales; but I still didn't take her advice. I figured we're already being punished; I had no interest in currying favour with our captors by dropping someone else in trouble. It might sound strange, but to me it was an integrity issue.

I later learned that, in prison terms, it was called being "staunch."

10th Letter

17th March

Dear Family and Friends,

I moved to Albion on the 11th of March. I have been here for a week and finally settled in.

Four of us travelled out in a prison van. This time, we were not hand-cuffed, because we had been classified as "non-violent, low risk."

The building was a very plain, split level, old boarding house with minor Tudor touches on the outside. We were processed and photographed for a new ID at the ground floor office, given a key to our own room and warned to keep it locked.

Moving inside, the downstairs area was dark and in need of fresh paint. It was dreary. My heart sank; it was the kind of place Justin and I used to inspect, give each other a look, and know exactly how we would renovate it.

I don't know what I expected. Perhaps something brighter and suggesting hope? Ugly wooden stairs led up to rooms that were at least, rooms and not cells. The beds were basic frames, the kind you see in second hand shops, with equally plain table and chair. There was no window in the door, this time, so at least there would be some privacy.

We arrived as lunch was laid out on a table. Simple enough, but to us it looked like a banquet. "Cheese!" In prison we had only been given two slices, a couple of times a week; now we could help ourselves.

The women were dressed in civilian clothes and were friendly enough. After lunch, I moved cautiously through the house to the rear yard. No wire fences. I lay along a picnic table bench-seat and stared at the sky. Lush foliage hung over me from a tree in the garden. I didn't want to move.

For some reason I felt disturbed.

I wanted to be happy; but it felt weird to have so little security, yet be just as much a prisoner.

Fortunately, in the afternoon Amanda returned from working at the cemetery and I felt much better for seeing her. She seemed brighter here.

I followed the advice of my more experienced criminal friends, back in S9, and have kept a low profile, while I "spy out the land." Just as well, because a few days into my stay, I was summoned for "the talk." It was to discuss what work I would do, and how I could be "rehabilitated"; but most of all, to discuss the "notes" that had been made about me and my faith.

During "the talk," I was warned to let the chaplains do the Christian work and keep my faith to myself.

A variety of answers filtered through my mind, none of which the supervisor would want to hear.

So far, the only "cheek" I had given was at Orientation on day 1. The officer handed us a booklet, with all the things we needed to know about Helena Jones Community Centre, and said, "This is your Bible!" I can't remember a training course where the manual has not been referred to as the Bible. *Yawn.* Before I could stop myself, I said, "So, like most people do with the Bible, we put it on the shelf and never read it?" *Hmm...*

Imagine if we'd had some Muslim women there and the officer said, "This rule book is the Koran!" It would be an outrage.

I was a little disturbed, for the first few days. There are two tiny babies and two toddlers here. I had to walk away from them because it made me miss my little daughters too much. I'm sure if I had watched that three-month-old baby girl for any longer, I would have started lactating!

I miss the friends I had made back at the prison, but the ladies here are nice. They are mostly here for fraud; some are drug addicts. Nobody is violent or dangerous. The atmosphere is less adrenalin-charged. They appear more "respectable." *Looks are deceiving.*

In the months preceding prison, several well-respected people had prophesied I would speak the right answer, in tricky situations, and I believe it could only be God sometimes. I wish I could share some of my more "colourful" stories; but as these letters are read by the guards, I don't want to get anyone in trouble. One young woman at the prison had asked me for a particular "favour." She was not someone you messed with. *She had asked me to have a visitor bring some drugs in for her.*

I looked at her in surprise and said vehemently, "There is no way in the world I would risk you getting into trouble!" She stared at me, and then burst out laughing. "Only you would be more concerned about me; anyone else would say "#%&* off! I'm not risking my neck for you!" she said.

Even though I didn't lead her to the Lord, we had a relationship of mutual respect.

As you know, Amanda is a Christian now. I had advised her to read Matthew and keep going to the end. She reported back to me that she has completed the New Testament, and would like to start at Genesis. I felt convicted, because I hadn't even read that much, though I had every intention of doing so…

Amanda also told me she had been having difficulties with one of the girls. I saw it myself, when I noticed someone sneering behind Amanda's back. Finally, something I could tackle here! I took Amanda's hands and we prayed for the girl. We prayed for God's blessings on every area of her life, repented of anger and resentment and for a good relationship.

As we finished, I told Amanda "I believe God will do something in less than twenty-four hours!" I don't normally put time limits on God, but He'd been moving quickly for me lately, so why not?

Well, less than one hour later, the girl found Amanda and apologised, asking if they could start fresh! Praise God.

Each new arrival must see the nurse. When my turn came, she asked me my age.

"Just turned forty," I answered.

"Ever had a mammogram?"

"No."

"Well Happy Birthday! I'll book you in for your first one."

Great!

At least all my medical care is free...what there is of it.

"Head count" as a roll-call, is every two hours from 6.30 a.m. to 6.30 p.m. A bell rings, and we assemble on one side, in the dining room, to answer the roll-call; just like school. As our name is called, we walk to the other side.

I have my own room now; but the door does not have a window in it, so during the night, again every two hours, an officer opens my bedroom door and sticks their head in, to see if I'm still there. I got a terrible fright, the first night, when I awoke to see a strange black male looking in at me! It's a reminder that I belong to them and I have no right to privacy.

I came home from work to discover all my things had been rifled through by officers. It was a disturbing reminder that my life is currently not my own; and privacy is an illusion.

The women here warned me to expect to be woken up at 4.30 a.m., for a surprise urine test.

Lovely!

They said I would have to pee in front of an officer, so I can be tested for drugs in my system. *Can't wait for that one!*

Work: The first couple of days, we were grading second-hand spectacles brought in by the Lions Club. They would be donated to third world countries. Each week, boxes of spectacles arrive; we clean them, then measure and record their power with a special machine. Finally, we seal them in boxes; ready to be picked up by the Lions Club representative. It's a wonderful cause. If you have a project that requires free labour, you can ask for an application form.

My job this week is at the cemetery. I will be paid $5.71 a day. We catch the train, wearing bright orange work shirts, overalls, steel-capped boots, and a big straw hat. *Very fetching!* We are not allowed to talk to anyone on the way.

To go to work meant stepping out of the grounds of the Centre. I paused at the edge of the car park, took a deep breath and stepped onto the footpath. I was out, in public. It felt peculiar and wrong. As we walked, I imagined a police car screaming to a halt in front of me, four burly officers jumping out and slamming me on the ground. "Where do you think you're going, Jenkins????"

It didn't happen. I meekly followed the other girls to the train station. However, once on the train, we realised we'd hopped on the WRONG ONE! We had accidentally got on the Caboolture train, instead of the one to Cleveland. My heart started racing in panic. Caboolture! We switched to the right train at the next station; but that lucky first one would continue on its way to my family's town. What a tease...

Each day, we tidy the graves, weed, mow and whipper-snip the edges. I discovered whipper-snipping is harder than it looks. Those of you who are acquainted with my relationship to hard physical work will understand, when I say they will get their $5.71 worth out of me.

I love "gallows humour," and swapped death jokes with the foreman. "There are never any customer complaints."

"Mobile phone reception isn't great, as there are too many dead spots."

The Cemetery is owned by the Catholic Church. I asked the foreman, if he ever wondered how many of the dead had gone to hell. *Oh come on, you do a lot of thinking while mowing, so don't be shocked!*

He said there was one fellow who turned up at a funeral just to "make sure the mongrel was really dead!"

There are above-ground tombs, and there are above-ground slots stacked high like the ends of bunks. Today, we waited for the supervisor in front of these cavities; some are filled and sealed, and some are just concrete rectangular holes.

The girls were getting spooked, imagining being inside one. I couldn't resist climbing into an empty one till my feet touched the far wall. They begged me to get out, so I slowly came forward making growly noises, and pulling scary faces, to freak them out! *It was fun.*

I'm not scared of death, although I'm not a fan of pain and suffering.

The Aborigines don't have to work at the cemetery, because according to their culture, they are not supposed to look at images of the dead. Many tombstones, especially the Italian ones, display a photograph of the dead person.

The cemetery dates back to the 1800's. Accordingly, the names on the oldest graves are Irish, then the next oldest are Italian, as per our mid-twentieth century immigration policy. As the Catholic requirement was lifted, more of the latter names sound Asian.

I am a historian, and I get caught up reading the etchings about the people, noting the family members who joined them later. Sadly, many gravesites only have us, to maintain them, as there are no family left to do it. Occasionally, vandals come in the night and damage the headstones. It makes us all mad.

By the way, I told the supervisor today that I wanted to die peacefully, in my sleep, like my grandfather... and not screaming in terror like his passengers! *(joke)*

I'll sign off now and be more spiritual next time. Mowing around graves gives me plenty of opportunity to receive jokes; I mean "words," from the Lord.

Love you all.

Trish xxxxx

11ᵗʰ Letter

Hello Family and Friends,

An odd thing happened yesterday morning. It was Sunday and I rose early, hoping to see some of the Hillsong Church program before the 6.30 muster call.

There were no toddlers around to claim the lounge TV for the cartoons, so I asked the girls sitting around if they minded me turning on the TV. "There are only cartoons on," they said.

"Hillsong is on Channel 10," I told them.

"Well, you can't have the TV on during muster." *Fair enough.* I raced upstairs to the other lounge, to put it on, and waited for the bell to summon me.

The roll-call proceeded without the bell, so I was the only one *not* present. My name was yelled up the stairs, so I sprinted back down. It seems the girls informed the officer that I was watching my "religious" show upstairs, as they didn't want to see it downstairs.

Well, the officer gave them all a "serve" about discrimination, and told them I was allowed to watch my show in the lounge like anyone else. No TV while muster is on, but either side of those five minutes, is fine.

How peculiar? I've no intention of manipulating the girls into watching my show, if they don't want to.

(Unfortunately, by sticking up for me, the officer inadvertently caused those women to resent me.)

Ironically, we had an impromptu sing-a-long last night, when I pulled out the guitar. We began with "Guns 'n' Roses," then ended with "Amazing Grace!" It's the one gospel song everybody knows, and a crowd had gathered by that time.

I'd like to collect the words and chords, to some of the lovelier choruses, because the women enjoy my singing and playing the guitar. Worship can touch the hardest heart.

I am enjoying my work at the cemetery. I like being around blokes for a change. There are four grounds men, one is our supervisor. On Friday, a hole, ("industry-speak" for "grave" apparently), was dug for a funeral. Its position was in between two existing monuments and, it had been dug a bit too close to one side!

It was hilarious watching the grounds men try to solve a rather serious problem!

There was not enough grass to sit the feet of the frame, which is used to support the coffin. We had visions of the coffin tipping off, and crashing into the hole, smashing the one already down there.

Graves often hold more than one coffin. Fortunately, by the time they worked out a solution, it was time for morning tea.

I do a lot of mowing. I mow in between the rows, and consider the names and dates on the tombstones. It's quite relaxing, and I compose great preaching messages in my head, based on what the Lord is showing me here.

Someone asked me once, given what I had learned, if I would do it all again.

"Of course not! I broke the law," I exclaimed. While I still would not "Do it all again," I have come to see that what I'm going through is worth it.

Many of us dream of having a great ministry; but we want it on our terms. We don't really count the cost because we cannot really see what the cost will be. Yet only by *willingly* paying the cost can we appreciate the joy and satisfaction of fulfilling our call.

One of my last conversations with Pastor Mark Ramsey was shortly before my sentencing. I told him that I was confident of a miracle; but there was a chance I could still go to prison.

"I don't want a prison ministry!" I half joked.

In that moment, I experienced conviction from the Holy Spirit.

The still, small voice asked me, *"Who does? Those women are just as important as anyone else, to me."*

I repented of my shallow selfishness. From that point, I quietly pressed into God about preparing me for incarceration. One thing I did ask Him was that it would be truly worth it, that I would not waste the experience. Not just one soul; but many.

Then, as now, my prayers were that I be effective.

Are you praying for provision for your ministry? Why not pray to be effective instead? The provision you really need, will be there, and your focus will be on the people who need YOU!

When we go out to work, our bags are searched. We can only take our lunch and a drink. No money, no book. We can't buy anything anyway. We cannot talk to the public or make a phone call. I had a piece of paper in my shirt pocket this morning. It had some notes I'd made on it.

"What's that in your pocket, Patricia?" asked the officer. Looking very guilty, I unfolded it, and handed it over.

"It's just a thought I wrote down…" 'Oh no, she'll really think I'm odd,' I thought.

She read it and, to my surprise, she gave it back.

My note was a topic I had been developing. It read as follows:

"Are you passionate about the work of the ministry? Or are you compassionate toward those whom the ministry is for?

Compassion will create Passion!

Passion without compassion is just ambition."

Someone wrote and asked if I were worried someone else would use my emails to create sermons; effectively "knocking off my message." If they did, I'd be flattered. It wouldn't be the first time a pastor has taken credit for someone else's gift... like Paul, I say, "If Christ be preached, who cares?"

I took two new girls out to the cemetery on Friday. I asked one if she has a partner on the outside. I was looking forward to seeing Justin on the weekend.

"I did have one for ten years; but she broke up with me. Her family is Christian, and she is trying to find God again, so she left me."

I know it's great to pray for the prodigal daughter to return; but I had never given any thought to the abandoned loved one, left behind. I prayed all day for this woman; I am still waiting on the Lord for an answer.

In the meantime, I am building a friendship with someone who knows I belong to the group which took her lover away.

This was my beautiful family in 2007.

From left: Olivia, Justin, Felicity, me, Chelsea.

The twins were 5 and Chelsea was 8.

At this point we had been through the liquidation; losing all our properties, cash and other investments, including our family home.

Justin and I were determined to keep things as normal as possible for our girls. He sold real estate and I began working for Phoenix Global, Australia's leading Corporate and Private Investigation Company.

Our earnings went to rent, maintaining lawyers and school fees. Our children's school environment was, and still is, more important than buying a house. Later, when we couldn't even pay rent, but boarded with my parents at Caboolture, we still made sure our children attended a good Christian school.

It was during this time I researched and wrote most of "Dangerous Wealth: What Every Successful Woman Needs to Know to Avoid Being Ripped Off!"

11th Letter, continued

Wednesday 25 March

I am feeling cranky and out of sorts this evening. About five little things, designed to humiliate *and* underline my powerlessness, combined to discourage me. Any *one* of them, I could shake off: from officers (blowing both hot and cold), about what I can take for lunch at the cemetery, to a particular supervisor who plays mind games to assert dominance.

Unfortunately, I play politics badly, and don't always provide the right answers.

It's like working for a corporation that has very strict guidelines; yet fails to inform all the managers and staff.

Just one example is the "form" our friends and family must fill out; to be able to visit. I received a message saying, I had to send one to a particular friend who had contacted the Centre, to ask what to do.

"Thank you. Where do I find the form?"

"On the forms rack in the dining room."

I looked and looked. No form. Back to the office. "There aren't any there; would you like me to top it up?"

"How many do you need?"

"One, please."

"Here"

"Thanks, but would you like me to put more in the forms rack?"

"No, they don't go on there."

"But..."

"You have to ask for them and you have to post them out."

"OK, thank you."

Shortly after this confusing interchange, Justin informed me that anybody can download the form from the Internet.

I was also summoned to answer a question about my mail.

"Have you asked for any religious paraphernalia to be sent to you?"

"No; but my friends may do that."

"So you never wrote to Kenneth Copeland Ministry asking for leaflets?"

"No I...hang on, I wrote to them, weeks ago, from the prison asking for a Bible! Has it arrived? Am I not allowed to have it?"

"Did you tell them you are a prisoner?"

"Probably."

"Did you misrepresent yourself as a chaplain?"

"No, of course not!"

"Well, what about this?" He presented an envelope to me with a flourish.

It was from KCM (Kenneth Copeland Ministries) addressed to Patricia Jenkins Care Prison Chaplains, BWCC.

I burst out laughing.

"Misrepresenting your identity is a serious matter. You should not be laughing!"

Oh dear.

I was never one to miss an opportunity, to dig the hole I'm in deeper. This time was no different!

I persisted, "It is funny, really. I wrote and told them that I had been praying for the ladies, and had introduced about fifteen of them to Jesus... They must have assumed I was in ministry, and actually, all of us are in ministry you know, every believer..." I babbled on. He wasn't impressed.

"We discussed specifically that you are *not* a chaplain, *did we not*?"

135

You know someone is asserting authority, when they use formal, old-fashioned syntax, such as "did we not," instead of "didn't we."

"Yes, but this was a letter from *before* that, and every believer is a minister. I was just doing what I ... there have been no complaints here..."

End of conversation.

That *would* have been an opportune time for me to be told that I was going to Warwick to work next Monday; but instead I hear it from others prisoners he had spoken to. *Whew! I'm not mad now; I see the funny side of this place.*

Everything I write to you, I must be prepared to explain to the supervisors, including the gentlemen referred to. Like many of the non-Christian authority figures, who are forced to address my faith, I believe there is an element of fear there. I suspect both he and the previous fellow I upset, at the prison, are mainstream "Christians" who don't really know what to do with someone who lives their faith unashamed, and with boldness.

The supervisor had said he was one; but wouldn't say which church he attended. It obviously wasn't my kind.

John 3:20 says "For everyone practicing evil hates the light and does not come to the light, lest his deeds be exposed."

A sincere Christian offends the nominal Christian, because the contrast in spiritual awakening is obvious. It's a problem for people who think they are better than you (i.e. not a criminal), to be confronted with an "inferior," who acts more like a Christian than they do.

The cemetery supervisor told me how important his Catholicism was to him. He was proud to be working for the Church in the Cemetery. He said he was part of a secret club of Catholics in strategic positions. It sounded much like Freemasonry to me.

If people are not Christians, I don't expect them to behave like one. If they are though, and they act differently, I will notice. I might even quietly challenge them on it even if it is only with a raised eyebrow.

The problem with telling me you are a practicing anything is that you know, I'll know, when you are being a hypocrite! When he used foul language, I said nothing, yet he could see I noticed the inconsistency of character. People hate that. A lowly criminal making you notice your own "sin," pricking your conscience? It was to become a problem for me down the track.

Ironically, even though the criminals here might not like the things of God, they do not treat me differently. I love them and they usually respond, each in their own time.

I remember a tall, intelligent black girl, who carried an air of authority, quietly sitting next to me. She said, "I've been watching you."

"Oh yeah?"

"Yes. You're not like anyone who comes through here. I don't agree with everything you say; but I can see you are sincere."

We became good friends after that. I later learned she was in for some serious stuff; which explained the other women's respect of her; and, possibly, their acceptance of me.

I am not good at clever, tricky conversations. I don't have the "savvy." I have to rely on the Holy Spirit, as anything I say can be misconstrued and have me in trouble. I could be "tipped" back to the prison, maybe put in S1 with the really bad girls, or even the D.U., something even worse.

Oddly enough, I don't fear that. I actually miss the feeling of being on the cutting edge, spiritually.

The spiritual opposition here is more insidious. I believe I need to pick up my warfare again, as it could be just as tricky. Please pray for wisdom and a strong anointing for me.

This place requires a different strategy. I will pray in tongues, more (not too obviously, as it could get me "tipped").

Some of the women here are not as rough as at the prison, but they can be quite nasty, behind people's backs.

I'm sensing it's time for me to take charge spiritually again. Once again, I pray blessings on those who annoy me.

I was right in sensing I should be on guard. I was too trusting, and did not see past the relatively "respectable" image some of the women portrayed.

I don't gossip, so I was not privy to the real spitefulness some of these smiling, middle-aged women directed at one another.

11th Letter, continued

Thursday 26th March

A good day today. I was informed that I am going to Warwick to work for the next ten days, from Monday. As for the letter from KCM, on closer inspection I realise they had written "CARE: Chaplain" In other words, it was for the chaplain to pass on to me! I was able to show that to the fellow who challenged me. I would have noticed it sooner, if I hadn't been flustered.

He acknowledged it, but not the hard time he had given me.

I was mad that the supervisor had made a mistake and scolded me for it. Prisoners are not entitled to the benefit of the doubt. It's always assumed we are in the wrong. I've never lived with perpetual disapproval before, it's quite demoralizing.

In any organization there can be leaders, or supervisors, who do not know how to accept being wrong. Instead they feel the need to save face, and twist things around, so it is still somehow your fault. It's a real attitude test, one that I failed this time...Of course, God was good enough to provide many such misunderstandings for me to practice on, during the time I spent at that place..!

Today, I whipper-snipped, mowed and used the leaf-blower. I discovered very quickly that it is best to blow in the same direction as the wind! The wind whistles through the tombstones and creates a wind tunnel.

At first, I couldn't start the blower. It turned out a hose had disconnected and, as I carried it back to the shed, I was bathed in petrol.

I also managed to expose the steel cap in my boot when I adjusted the height of the lawn mower. My boots are a bit big and my toe slipped under the side. You guessed it; the blade sliced the toe of my boot....and that's why we have Workplace Health and Safety procedures!

Turn it off, before adjusting it, Trish!

Fun and games...

We had two funerals close together, this week. As the first party left, we raced out to disassemble the framework around the grave with its lovely curtains, and ran it over to the next hole. It's an odd feeling; lifting the coffin with pulleys, in order to slide the ribbon-like ropes out.

One girl's hat blew off, and it passed over the grave. It's lucky we didn't have to climb down inside to retrieve it!

Anyway, stay tuned for the next episode of "Perils of Patricia".

If you would like to visit me, just contact Justin. You can download a form from the internet. It could take up to eight weeks for the form to be "processed."

I finally got to see Justin and our girls, over the weekend; which was really special. I'm glad the girls can visit me here, in a nice garden, with me in normal clothes. The twins think I am "helping some ladies."

Love to all, Trish

Eventually the twins asked me directly, if I were in jail. They had overheard things, as children often do. I said, "Yes, it's 'time out' for grownups, just like children have time out, when they do the wrong thing."

12th Letter

15th April

Hello friends,

Sometimes I wonder if I can stay positive for another six months. Sometimes I despair at the injustice of my situation; but then I choose to remind myself that I am here, because the Lord has placed me here for a purpose, and I will fulfil that purpose. It's the regular humiliations, of being "put in my place," that are painful.

Then, I remind myself of John Bevere's teaching on submission. It's hard. It helped, when one of the girls said, "Well, we are criminals and this is the price we pay."

I am reminded of being a helpless schoolgirl, under the authority of teachers who alternately joke and then threaten. Just as you relax, you cross some unwritten boundary and get snapped at. I hate that feeling of powerlessness.

It must be how many Indigenous people feel, or perhaps those who, by virtue of poverty or handicap, must rely on the grace of an arbitrary authority. No wonder God is passionate about defending the poor and dispossessed. He knows human nature can't be trusted to do so.

I think about the property boom differently now. So many bought up property in low income areas, increased the rent, and poorer families were driven further out. Then, some of these investors shamelessly boast of God's blessing on their lives. Makes you wonder.

Justin and I were probably too soft on our tenants, but we cared about them as families. Each Christmas, we bought a gift and let them know they were appreciated. One couple wrote us a reference for future tenants, when they left!

My life is still much better than most. I have a wonderful husband, a supportive family and a sense of "destiny." There is purpose in my life. This morning, I spent time in the Word, waiting on the Lord. I went to work with a sense of joy and peace.

Twelve of us were bussed out to Warwick on Monday (30th March) to do community work. Moving is unsettling. Along with a different bed, you have different people around you with all their hang ups and attitudes.

One lady was particular bitchy and bossy, and I was ready to say to her, "Look, I'll ignore what I've heard about you, if you do the same for me!" Fortunately, I chose to pray for her instead. As always when I do what I know is right, instead of what I'd like, things were fairly civil.

Day 1: For the first day, we worked sorting clothes at a St Vincent de Paul warehouse. The volunteers there were very welcoming. It's a warehouse where we sort out donated second hand clothes.

Day 2: We cleaned up the showgrounds, where this weekend's International Polocrosse Championships will be held. I cleaned cobwebs down from a large shed, and surveyed the filthy floor. Never one to exert unnecessary energy, I thought 'why sweep when you can blow?'

I employed my best leaf blowing techniques to chase dirt and grass clippings out the roller doors. Much of it blew up and back into my hair, and through my clothes, but it was fun and more satisfying than using a broom!

Day 3: I managed to get on the list of girls for the St Vincent de Paul retail shop. At last my field, sales and marketing. These I do know how to do! I am not allowed to talk to the customers; but we can answer their queries by directing them to the staff.

It sounds simple enough; wouldn't you think?

While I rearranged the books, a gentleman asked me about a particular author. Before he knew it, he was happily purchasing several books by my favourite authors. I ask you, "Who can stay silent with Jeffrey Archer's *'Not a Penny More, Not a Penny Less,'* shouting from the shelf?"

In the afternoon, I moved to the toy section and regrouped them in colours and styles. Somehow two brightly-coloured educational pieces found their way to the counter, in the arms of a middle aged lady. The satisfaction I felt was absurd. Not being allowed to talk to the public can be awkward; but we can't be rude, can we?

I remember waiting at the train station last week, after working at the cemetery, for the return trip to Albion. A lady with her arm in a sling asked me to help her locate the ticket machine, so I took her over to it. I felt uncomfortable. *REMEMBER, WE ARE NOT TO TALK TO ANYONE!*

Then I had to work out her fare for her. Finally, I nearly fainted, when she flipped open her wallet and asked me to take the money out for her. My eyes drifted up to the security cameras, as I warily reached in past the $20 and $10 notes to fish out the required coins.

Phew!

The first thing I did, upon returning to the Albion house, was report what happened. The Department of Corrections sometimes actually puts *dummy* travellers on the trains, to see if we will talk to them. That's your taxpayer dollars at work!

Back at Warwick, I have ten friends and a couple of the girls I like well enough. The rest are quite cliquey and I don't particularly feel warm towards them. When they sit around, they gossip about whoever isn't there.

I am mindful of my church friends' attitude to gossip. I like that anyone of us can say, "Hold on, is this starting to sound like gossip?" and we modify the conversation. I miss the Friday night Girls group I attended. It's a great friendship group, and an example of having a fun, bonding, talkative time, without gossiping. I am lonely for those friends.

Our Queenslander house sits on the edge of the Warwick Showgrounds and Amanda and I have been running around the oval, each afternoon. There are horse-jumps set up, so I thought, 'What the heck?' I hurdled over the low ones, not realising I was entertaining the women in the "smoking" group and providing them with more gossip material. Apparently, one of my friends gave them all a serve, for being bitchy about me. But, if I didn't hear it, I don't care.

I should have cared. I should have remained invisible, not drawn attention to myself. That handful of older women was to make my life a misery.

This afternoon however, I sat outside and chatted with the Lord.

"I don't particularly care for these women, Lord. I prefer the ones from prison, at least they were colourful. These are just dried up sour pusses. I have no interest in them, or being any more than polite to them."

Then, the Lord showed me them individually. Each one was his daughter. I felt a pang of remorse. I prayed wryly, "I want people to care about, and like, my daughters; why would you be any different?"

So, I found myself repenting of my attitude, AGAIN!! As I write, I am shaking my head and laughing at myself. I prepare, once again, to care for people who are not particularly nice, and may, in fact, dislike me. I may look foolish temporarily; but I always win *this* game.

I was reminded of my own revelation, "Compassion creates Passion." My antipathy will disappear, when I think compassionately. Then my compassion will make me passionate about these women.

Once again, it will be worth it.

12th Letter continued

Sunday 5th April.

After I wrote the last paragraph I had a disturbing couple of days. It was serious enough that I didn't tell my family because I didn't want them to worry about me. I knew it would take longer than overnight to win over these nasty older women. They are in their forties and fifties.

Most women I know in that age group are at least polite. These women have the culmination of years of pain and bitterness riding on their shoulders without knowing much grace. Their longevity and hard work is the only thing that gives them a sense of value. Life must be very frightening for them.

Well, I found out that the officer (looking after us), told them off for discriminating against me. They immediately thought I had complained; something you don't do in prison. *Of course, it doesn't stop them from doing it.* While they stopped being openly hostile, I still get the cold shoulder.

I prayed on and off, all night, asking the Lord to bless them, and their families, their jobs, their finances, and to soften their hearts.

The next day, I was left home with the ringleader. Something had changed. We chatted and I swore I had not spoken to the officer. She answered stiffly, "I never said you did!"

My reply was, "Well, that would be my first thought in your position." I was mortified. "I just want to get along and do my time just like you do." We made cakes together and she showed me how to make butter icing for them. Another battle won.

Or so I thought.

One of the bitchy things they did was not just to me. Five of them live in "dongas" (Portable rooms) next to the house and connected by a veranda. They have a separate bathroom, while the rest of us live inside the house. The gas to the house ran out, which meant no hot water. The next morning, the outside women claimed to have no hot water either.

They just didn't want to share; even though they had finished their showers. One of their friends stays in the house, and used their bathroom claiming, "Ooh yes, it was freezing!!"

My roommates guessed they were lying; but I couldn't condemn, without evidence. I quietly slipped into their bathroom and ran the hot tap. Sure enough, it was nice and warm. Too late for me though, I'd had my cold shower. I said nothing; but they were found out, and the supervisor was furious.

I just shook my head. I really don't understand that kind of childish selfishness, in grown women. I actually felt embarrassed for them, because everyone knew.

Oddly, by the end of the day, they were all friends again, laughing and talking. All was forgiven. I wonder if their easy acceptance is because we've *all* done the wrong thing, and not in a position to hold a grudge, or that kind of poor behaviour just goes with the territory, so it's no big deal.

I've seen this, many times, in prison. They seem to get over each other's bad behaviour much more easily than people on the outside, including church.

I thought I, too, had been extended this "forgiveness" and acceptance.

I should have known better.

I happened to mention that I had made a list of everybody's names, to help me remember them. I couldn't resist adding that I then prayed for each one to have a good safe day. I hoped that they would appreciate the gesture. *Instead, it set the cat among the pigeons!*

A list is a symbol of power. Prisoners are on all kinds of lists, few of them, voluntarily. While nobody told me to my face, it got back to me that they were gossiping and, dramatically expressed feeling "violated."

Others thanked me for my thoughtfulness and for caring.

Anyway, I offered to cross anyone off the list; which made them feel better. I'm still going to pray for them anyway; but I left that bit off.

Fortunately, after my day making cakes (with that particular one), all seemed to fall into place, and I was treated relatively normal. It was quite a relief. I'm not so naïve that I will trust any of them; but it really goes to show how powerful praying for your enemies is.

Instead they plotted to get me kicked off the Warwick team.

On to happier things: I absolutely love Polocrosse! It's like Polo but with Lacrosse racquets. It killed me that I couldn't have a ride on one of those magnificent Quarter horses, but I did get a chance to stroke one or two. Placing my face against a big cheek and breathing that lovely horsey smell was an instant high. One gently nuzzled my hand, with his soft lips, and I nearly cried with longing. This was a universe I had no access to.

Only a fellow "horsey" person could understand what I felt.

I didn't mind the work at all. I felt like a normal volunteer; except we are not allowed to handle money. Friday night, I served meals; Saturday, I cleaned toilets and picked up rubbish; Sunday was food preparation and washing up. Monday, we gave all the grounds and buildings a thorough clean, and we were all heartily sick of one another, by then.

One woman asked me if I could put someone on the top of my prayer list, because, "she's a two-faced #$&* who is really #$&*ing me off right now!"

Okay....

There is a young Christian woman here, a charismatic Islander, who is in for Centrelink (Welfare) fraud. Most of the "fraudies" are single mothers, in for ripping off Centrelink. She whispers to me privately; but the rest of the time she joins the others.

She is terrified church people will find out she has been in prison.

My parents know some relatives of hers, and even *her* parents' needed assurance that *mine* wouldn't say anything.

Shame makes us hide our sin. Just like Adam and Eve hiding from God, so He wouldn't think less of them, we do the same.

Some bosses manage their staff by promoting a culture of "control by tattling." It's counterproductive and undermines team work.

The women, back at the prison, warned me that people who went to Helena Jones were all "dogs." That means, they tell the officers things about other prisoners, in order to curry favour. Colouring it up is even more effective.

I understand the officers' need to know, if someone is being bullied or taking drugs; but it became clear to me that those who wanted to be in control of the other women, did so, by getting them into trouble. That's something I found repugnant.

This woman was later used, by the others, to get me into trouble. Later, she made a complaint about me that got me kicked off the Warwick team.

The irony was she still trusted me, as a Christian, not to blow her secret to the outside world. Another painful attitude and temptation for me to overcome...!

While working away, I am reminded of other things. Chopping the lettuce, I heard the voice of a very dear, baker friend who taught me how to cut bread without squashing it, "Let the knife do the cutting, Trish. You don't have to make an effort."

The word of God is a double-edged sword; not just the word, but the Spirit, too. If only we were more skilled at letting the Sword of the Spirit cut for us. I am practicing saying nothing overt; but just praying for these women.

So often, we try to make things happen without using discernment. That is not to say we never need to speak boldly;

we do. However, it works best, after we have honestly spent time with the Lord. Then, as the scripture says, "When you open your mouth I (God) will fill it."

Without the Holy Spirit prompting, all we give is our opinion.

I really admire my husband's Catholic family. They accept one another, warts and all. There is a lot of love, in the family, even though they don't talk much about it.

They think I'm a little odd in my style of faith (unfortunately, Protestant); but they have been very good to me. I love them.

Someone said this experience would show me who my real friends were. I've discovered I have a lot of wonderful friends. My parents have had the same discovery, with some surprising disappointments.

Still, most people have been very encouraging, and I thank you all for your interest in our journey.

Journal notes

6th April (Very late).

Sometimes I feel like we are pets. Not the kind loved by a family; but more like working farm dogs.

We work, because that is what we are here for.

We are fed, when the bell rings.

We assemble to be counted. We cannot be trusted, so we stand silently, waiting for our name to be called. We answer, "Yes," and walk across the room to prove we are here.

When we need medical attention, it is dispensed, so we can get back to work.

Our lives are managed.

Our light and TV must be turned off, by 10.30 p.m. Every two hours, someone opens our door to check that we are still here.

It's like someone else owns us; we have no individual value. We are stripped of all qualifications and experience. The assumption is that we are stupid. Even the man who delivers the glasses made a comment, and felt the need to add, "That was an adjective." *Who does that?*

My quiet response was, "Far be it from me, to correct your dangling participles *thoroughly*. 'Thoroughly' is an adverb, by the way, it describes 'how'." My voice trailed off, and I sensed a shift in his assessment of me.

Why should I have cared? Why did I feel the need to show him I probably knew more about the English language than he? Even if what I said was rubbish, he wouldn't have been able to tell. I too, used to assume people in prison lacked intelligence, "mad scientists" notwithstanding…

"Occasionally, I hear comments along the lines of, "Well, that's what happens when you go to jail. You should have thought of that, before you broke the law!"

In the past I, myself, had no problem with having this attitude about people in jail.

I have lost the right to personal dignity. I practice submission on a level that degrades me, yet I must play the game. We are treated like naughty children, at a cold, callous boarding school, without the respect. Is my pride so great? Why is this *stripping of my self-respect* so hard to accept?

We talk of humbling ourselves, lest we be humbled. Here, I carefully summon humility, before speaking with any officer; lest they humiliate me. It's my choice, to do it first.

"My choice." One of the few, yet not really a choice; it's more of a sensible strategy.

I think of Paul, a willing prisoner in chains, and I feel ashamed of my complaints. That man could have avoided prison. He would have been released had he not insisted on having his case heard before Caesar. Yes, we know the bigger picture was that it extended the audience of the Gospel; but I wonder about the man.

Did he ever look back and miss the comfort of his previous life? The personal choices he could make? He says he counts all his previous privileges as rubbish (Philippians 3:8).

Paul mentions various emotions we can all identify with: Loss, despair, pain. I have my comforts here. What I suffer most is mental. In a world of equality for sex, race and religion, an "offender" is consciously and deliberately debased. Those rights are gone.

It's easy to claim those rights are restored, when a person completes a sentence; but they are not. Their future is damaged, in two ways. First, a criminal record affects a person's employability. Second, the damage done to a person's emotional and mental stability when they have been treated this way undermines every rehabilitation and education program.

I wonder about my own ability to maintain a healthy perspective, when it is so contrary to the prevailing pressures.

Oh Paul, how did you do it? It was harder for you, and yet you had so much more spiritual drive, than I. I'm not writing the Bible. My little messages may not even be of interest.

For now though, I can still pray to be effective. I can practice spiritual disciplines from Matthew 6. I can control what I eat; well, I can choose not to eat what is served. I am in control of my thoughts. There is purpose in this experience. Most of all, I can at least treat people like they matter, because they do. There are several young women, who are drawn to me, because of it.

I will not despair and feel sorry for myself; at least, not for long.

Lord, you are the "One who lifts my head." (Psalm 3:3). Only your opinion matters. May I be worthy of this suffering. Let me not squander it. Amen.

I want to weep, ashamed of my self-pity, my softness. I try not to think about the significance of a criminal record blighting my life, for all my life.

The words of "Kurtz" (in Joseph Conrad's *"Heart of Darkness"**) come to mind, *"The Horror, the Horror!"*

Then I heard the Lord whisper, *"The Privilege..."*

Ah, sweet perspective - a perspective too significant not to meditate on. Lord, show me the full meaning of why this is a privilege, and I will relish the experience. I can endure any hardship, if you let me see it is worth it.

* Joseph Conrad's novella, "Heart of Darkness," *was later made into the disturbing film classic,* "Apocalypse Now" *with Marlon Brando as Kurtz.*

12th letter, continued

Thursday 9th April

We got back to Albion yesterday. As we were driven through the city, I remember arriving at Albion the first time, in a prison truck. Would I feel sad? No. As soon as I entered the house, I was welcomed by my friends. It felt so different to what I had been coping with. I realised, I really had been ostracised, out at Warwick.

Well, I'm stronger now and older. I no longer feel like it's my job to placate people. I know how to take charge of the situation spiritually.

I might be in custody; but I'm no more a prisoner than anyone else in a restricted situation. What is *your* situation? Is *your* prison a bad marriage? Are *you* in a dead–end career? Suffering depression or sickness? Wherever you are, your prison *is in your head*.

You can control what you think about.

Like Paul, I have learned how to abound, and how to be abased (like now). I have learned to be content, because I am really only a willing captive of Christ, and He loves me.

In spite of the irritations and behaviour of others, I do not feel like a prisoner in my heart. Perhaps they sense this, and it irks them? I feel like a visitor, passing through, with the Holy Spirit as my tour guide. This attitude allows me to rise above any persecution, and actually care for the people around me. Even the officers are more trapped than I am. I must confess to a fleshly satisfaction, at this thought.

I have no razor wire holding me here, at Albion; but officially I am a prisoner. You may have no razor wire; but you may feel more like a prisoner than I do.

Take heart. A genuine relationship with Jesus, who really loves you and is vitally interested in your life, will set you free.

Thank you, to those who write to me. It gives me such encouragement to hear from you. Justin always prints out your emailed replies and posts them to me, as well.

God bless you all with health, prosperity, great relationships and the revelation of Himself to you.

Love,

Trish

13th Letter

12th April

Easter Sunday,

Hello family and friends,

Happy Easter! I know you won't receive my salutation on the day, but this is close enough. I can set my TV to turn on, like an alarm, in the morning. It enables me to be up and dressed, before the 6.30 a.m. muster.

This morning, to my delight, I recognised Daniel K singing for Wesley Mission, live at the Opera House! If you know Daniel and Jody, please let them know how I am going and what a blessing he was to me by singing, "The Great Southland of the Holy Spirit."

I really enjoy some of the younger women here. These Generation Y girls are still cheerful, trendy and fun. They love to help me get prettied up for visits with Justin. I realised all my T-shirts are square, boxy things, so they loaned me some pretty little tops. Apparently I was also wearing my jeans way too high, making my bum look bigger than it was.

They delighted in adjusting them for me. One of them reached forward and yanked the waist down to my hips. Then another produced a pen that she plunged down my front pockets. Upon removal, she explained, "This is how you keep the pockets flat." *Right. Got it!*

Resisting the urge to "hoik up" my pants, I suddenly realised why a tattoo, on my lower back, would not be out of place! Or another peeping above the band where an appendix scar would go!

"Good thing I've never had a Caesarean," was all I could say!!!

Don't worry! I'm exaggerating. It just *felt* that way!

I definitely felt more "groovy," and it lifted my spirits.

Non-Christians ask what my plans are, for when I get out. Christians ask what my vision is, and what I think my time here is preparing me for.

I have a vision for when I am released. What I am becoming and learning here is not just for me; but for the greater body and the secular community. However, this is not just a school; it is my ministry now.

I am not waiting for release, or a signal of some kind, to tell me when I am ready to start. I started the moment I was led downstairs from the courtroom to the dungeons... sorry...to the "cells," below.

This is my field and my ministry, for now. It's partly about my growth; but wholly about serving Him here by serving others.

Are you waiting for a signal? Are you waiting for finance to enable you to "go forth?" Are you, like the fifty-seven-year-old woman I talked to, waiting for a pastor to say you are ready? This lady had a vision all her life, to work with little brown children, teaching them, and helping in a village somewhere.

She was waiting for the Lord to tell her she could go. In the meantime, she was a valued member of a church; but her pastors said she wasn't "ready." What rubbish!

I said to her, "You are fifty-seven, with a brain, and your own resources. If you are passionate about going and teaching little brown kids to read, then go! The God I know won't mind!!!"

Do what you are able to do; but don't expect others to be as excited as you are about it, and don't expect them to support you financially. God will provide for what He has called you to.

Bono, from U2, was interviewed by Bill Hybels, and said, "Instead of asking God to bless what you are doing, find out what He is already blessing, and do that!"

It's so simple, yet so powerful. Whatever you do; do something. Do it; without expectation or resentment or self-righteousness; and at all times, be prepared to give it up, because it is never yours.

I gave up everything; well, it was taken; but I was always mindful that it was God's, not mine. I have no resentment about my losses and have been blessed by the unexpected gains in my current situation.

13ᵗʰ Letter, continued

13ᵗʰ April Monday Evening

I commenced a Certificate II in Hospitality, today. I figured I'd do any courses on offer, even if it meant missing the public holiday. I agreed to this one, with some reservations. I knew we would cover hygiene and food preparation. This would mean being exposed to the many horror stories of maggots in fast food outlets. Can I ever risk fast food again, knowing the risk I am taking? *Sure I can.*

You have to understand that, from in here, a McDonald's burger looks mighty good.

In the same way, I sometimes regret all the customer service training I've done. It means I can't help but notice its glaring absence, often much to the embarrassment of my companions. Ignorance sometimes really is bliss. I suppose "wisdom" knows when to speak up and, when to let it slide.

I'm learning when to stand my ground, and when to yield. While at Warwick, two of my room-mates, kept passing wind, and laughing uproariously.

Finally, I asked if they could go out of the room, to "break wind," as it was rude, and the rest of us shouldn't have to suffer. One of them simply said, "No."

I tried again. "Look, you filthy animal, have some respect, and break wind outside!"

She laughed at me. "Trish, get it right, it's a fart! Use the proper term! It is fart! Fart! Fart! What the hell is 'break wind'?"

At that, I gave up and we both fell about laughing. Thank God she gets out this week! She will be replaced by the burping brigade. These are my young Gen Y friends who could sound a gong just by belching near it!

You guys really don't know what you're missing... really...!

I smile as I remember, back at the prison, watching two tough women play Scrabble. To watch, and not correct spelling, was exercise in self-control (and wisdom!) Only an idiot would try.

(E.g. There is no x in "ask," as in "Arx a question!")

Same letter, continued

14th April Tuesday evening...

This afternoon, a handful of us were treated to a Sexual Health talk. Apparently, I needed to brush up on sexually transmitted infections.

It's assumed that upon release we will burst out of here, abuse substances, and forget how to "choose wisely," when it comes to men.

I saw a huge cultural-gap yawn open, and I thanked God for my marriage.

Back at the prison, sugar and butter were rationed to each table, but we ran out quickly. So I learned to live without sugar, butter, full-cream milk, my family, *and* my privacy. Now, thanks to the Sexual Health talk, I was cruelly reminded of other fun things I am living without!

Thank you for your letters. It makes me feel normal and *connected*, to hear about the everyday things going on. One of the letters mentioned the "Colour Conference," which would have been fantastic. "Colour" is a massive, women's conference, hosted by Hillsong Church in Sydney.

Maybe I'll be able to go next year?

Another friend of ours had been to the Colour Conference. She told me how she wished she could be one of the speakers. Then she felt the Lord ask, "And what would you say?"

Well, she might have had messages for a certain level then, but now she is in Uganda with her husband, who is rebuilding a hospital that was destroyed during the civil conflict.

My friend is creating her "message," just as I am. I had joked with her about her hardship at least being honourable and noble. Mine is not something I can be proud of. Of course, the Lord has never hesitated to help me squash my pride.

Ironically, I reckon I am a lot more comfortable than she is right now.

The dinner bell rings and, like "Pavlov's dogs," we troop into the dining room, trained to expect food. No physical privations here.

Whatever you are doing; your life is your message. Maybe it's not for a platform in front of thousands; maybe it is for your playgroup, your business associates, and your family.

Remember that, first and foremost, your "message" is for you.

If your message does not change *you* for the better, well then, perhaps you need to give it a bit more thought and prayer.

So many want to speak to thousands; but few realise the price that may be paid, to earn the scars required, for that kind of platform.

I told God, I didn't want a "Joseph" experience. I'd settle for something less than being "2IC" of Egypt. I told Him, I really don't care sufficiently, for His people, to endure the suffering I might face!

Now, I believe the suffering is worth it, to see the great results. I still don't want to be 2IC of Egypt. I'm happy with wherever He decides to put me - now and later.

I've learned to be content.

Love to all.

Your friend, Trish

Journal notes

15th April

In some ways, unbelievers are far more judgmental than Christians. We at least understand temptation, the influence of the devil, and his ability to create the "perfect storm," so we fail. However, we also understand grace and repentance (at least theoretically.)

What I'm observing is the hypocrisy of someone judging anyone whose morals are lower than their own; but their own bar is not set very high! I don't get it; except to go back to the instinctive need for a person, who has low self-esteem, to look down on someone.

In prison, many women are critical of prostitutes, yet there are plenty of them here. A drug addict generally has three choices for obtaining drugs, when the habit gets expensive.

1. Deal drugs to get drugs
2. Prostitute herself to get drugs
3. Become the girlfriend of a drug dealer to get drugs

Apparently it is more respectable to deal drugs than sell sex to get them. I don't understand that thinking.

I met a very sweet, young woman who was here for drug trafficking. She described how she, and her husband, slid into that world. It was somehow a bit more exciting than alcohol at a party...

You wouldn't pick her for an addict. She was a respectable, middle-class wife and mother, yet her life was taken over. Now, she has a strong resolve go straight... You hear that a lot.

...Another lovely friend pointed to someone in the newspaper. He was one of the "Joe Public" who'd been asked a survey question. He looked like a nice, respectable fellow. "I sold him a lot of drugs over time!" She said.

Ordinary people.

The Urine Test

Urine drug tests are done periodically; but I'd not had one here yet. One of the courses we did finished at lunchtime.

I'd had a couple of coffees, at morning tea, and the next session was a long one. I was busting for a wee, so I dashed upstairs to the bathroom as soon as we were let out. What a relief!

Then, I was summoned to the office.

"U.T. Jenkins!" *Uh oh.*

The procedure is usually done on known drug users; but apparently, there is a box needing a tick, to ensure everyone is done. I was given a bowl, and told to sit on the toilet and wee in it. An officer watched from the open doorway. She didn't stare, she was just there to make sure I didn't... well I don't know, would I carry a cup of clean urine around, as a "just in case" measure?

The drug addicts are used to it, and are usually awakened at 4 a.m. to "produce." The rule is that *to not produce any urine* is an offence. You have sixty minutes to provide a wee, and if you can't, or don't, you will be "tipped back" to the prison.

Well, in my case, I had just completely emptied my bladder, and NOTHING was happening!

"Come on Jenkins."

How embarrassing, for both of us!

I was allowed to go and drink some water, under supervision, of course. I downed five glasses and waited a few minutes, to try again.

Ten minutes passed; still nothing.

"They call it 'shy bladder,' when you can't produce while being watched." One of the officers told me helpfully, "Don't worry, it'll come."

My bladder must have been very shy, or very dry.

Twenty minutes passed. Nothing else passed.

They had other people to test, so I was allowed just outside the glass office door, where they could still keep an eye on me.

Ever the creative thinker, I began to wonder if I could speed up the process by getting my blood pumping. I started jumping up and down, much to the amusement of the other women; hoping gravity would help the effort.

Forty minutes.

Normally, since having my twins, such jumping would be a hazard. Surely, that would help things now?

Nope.

I was, however, providing entertainment, for the women in the unit who came out to watch and giggle. It was very funny; but also serious, because even though I have no drug history, they would have no choice, but to tip me back to prison if I could not produce.

In my head, I knew my body would do what it should, in the time given; but it was still a worry.

I was eventually the last one tested.

Finally, with a few minutes to the deadline, enough emerged for the test. I had made a hilarious spectacle of myself; but I was deemed "clean."

I mustered my dignity and stalked back inside. On the inside,

I was glad to have made a few people smile.

Journal notes

16th April

I got in trouble again.

Someone complained that they felt I was too "familiar," and they felt "uncomfortable." The bathroom is at the end of the hall. After showering, I had walked back to my room with a towel around me. I stopped outside my door to chat briefly with another woman, before disappearing into my room. I'm not the only one who has ducked back to her room, from the bathroom, in just a towel. We are all women upstairs; except when officers do the nightly headcounts.

The officers said that it seemed apparent to everyone but me, that this is a workplace, not my home, and I should be sensitive to others. I was being too familiar.

I must have looked puzzled, because they said, "You talked to someone, while standing in your towel."

"Too familiar?" I asked. "I don't touch people, and I don't talk about personal issues. OK, I get the towel thing, and thanks for telling me again about the need to behave like this is "the office." (Even though I live here?)

They looked uncomfortable. *Clearly, I still didn't get it.*

I said, "There were no men around, we are all women, and I wasn't showing anything. It's not like a man was... well, I suppose there are women here who have *tendencies*... oh!" My eyes widened, and I finally understood *what* they were saying *without saying it.*

Still being a bit slow, I bought into their politically correct bulldust, and agreed that I should be sensitive to those who found women attractive. "Obviously, I wouldn't do it, if they were a man..." It was only afterwards that I wondered why *I* was the one who had done something inappropriate, when officially, the lesbian thing doesn't happen here.

165

Then I got mad. The woman could have said, "Hey, do you mind? Remember, I'm gay," instead of running to the officers. You wanna act like a man? A man wouldn't do that. Pathetic.

She did manage to tell everyone else though.

Don't tell me I've got an attitude, Pal!

It actually took me a day to work out who it was. Even then, someone had to point out that a lady in my hallway, who was a lesbian, thought I was giving her "signals!"

Goodness me! I don't treat anyone differently. If she were a man then, of course, I would behave differently; but she's not. She was quite likeable, in a big "canteen-lady-who-carries-the-heavy-things" way. The "tomboy" in me could relate to her; or so I thought.

She'd said that she missed the intellectual conversations she had, with another educated woman, back at the prison. I, too, enjoyed talking about ideas, instead of gossip. It reminded me that the world was still turning out there. Talking to another educated person meant I didn't always have to explain what I meant or risk someone feeling patronised, because I wasn't speaking simply enough.

Anyway, I found her and apologised. I had already told her I was "straight," and assumed that set the boundaries. Hmm. It seems, even in feminist Lesbian Land, the "object of desire" gets the blame, and shoulders the responsibility for the other person's lust problem! How irritating that it was no different to a man claiming, "She led me on!"

Irk! I don't fancy being the object of anyone's lustful desires in here!

It's disappointing, because I enjoyed her conversation and wit; but I won't be risking that again. It's such a shame. The irony is that I never had a problem with men thinking I was "giving signals."

Men never pestered me; even when I wanted them to!

I just can't do the femme fatale thing, never could. Ah well... on the inside I find the situation hilarious. Now, I have the wicked urge to mess with her head, give her a wink...maybe blow her a little kiss... ha, ha... but I won't of course.

Another irony was, the officers knew what they were referring to; but I didn't, and they knew I didn't. The significance of it was over my head! How awkward for them.

How funny that they clearly felt awkward!

Well, it reminds me of Titus 1:15

> "To the pure, all things are pure, but to those who are corrupted and do not believe, nothing is pure. In fact, both their minds and consciences are corrupted."

So why am I the one apologising?

Journal notes

Another day...

I wonder about a lot of things. I ask why, what does it mean? What does it say about a person, about society? How can things be better? For example, I asked an officer why we were referred to as "offenders." I understand that we committed an offence; but who am I offending now? Am I offensive?

She suggested it was "politically correct."

I then asked, "How's that? Being labelled an 'offender' hardly encourages rehabilitative thinking."

She wondered why I would even ask. Of course, she didn't know.

They do monthly reports on us, which we are supposed to 'sign off,' on. I suspect they have two sets of reports; one we must see, and another *they don't wish us to see*. I have no interest in their opinion of me. I don't need to impress anyone in order to get parole. I am relieved I don't have to play that game.

I was asked to sign off on a report that suggested I had "Cognitive distortion."

"What do you mean by that?" I asked.

"Well, cognitive refers to the brain and..."

"I know what the words mean; but why have you used them about me?" I interrupted.

"Well you just don't think like everyone else! You come out with things that are different."

I answered, "Yes, I do see things differently to everyone else... and the problem is...?"

"You question things other people don't worry about. You don't see things the way they are." She was struggling. I didn't let her off the hook; but perhaps I should have.

"Who says that's the way they are?" I persisted.

"Well, you don't have to sign it if you don't agree with it."

Cognitive distortion! A politically correct way to say I'm a bit crazy. Who is really the crazy one in a mad house?

Why on earth would I want to think the same way as these people?

Officers, staff and official visitors often assume prisoners are stupid and uneducated. Someone who doesn't fit the mould can make them uncomfortable. One of them made a comment, looked at me patronisingly and explained, "That means…" It was something quite banal.

Again! My inner Smart Alec popped up. I raised an eyebrow and calmly replied, "Well, that's axiomatic!" The look on his face was priceless.

The "cognitive distortion" claim was a different kind of irritation. I made the officer work for it.

"Is thinking like everyone else here a good thing? How do you know my perspective is wrong? Perhaps I am not the one with a distorted view of things. Perhaps I am a normal person not fitting into the abnormal environment here."

I looked at her and said, "Being a Christian will give me a different perspective. I'm glad I think differently."

She was a nice lady doing her best; but she was uncomfortable. "Well you can refuse to sign it," she repeated.

Perhaps, I should have shut my mouth, again.

No doubt she would have another report to prepare.

Asking different questions was how my husband and I became successful. It's what entrepreneurs do.

In the right environment, it is stimulating, leads to progress, productivity, innovation, problem solving, and creates an exciting future.

In the wrong environment, it makes you a pain in the neck!

14th Letter

27th April

Hello All,

I've had some great victories and great challenges. Twice I was asked to pray for someone's parole to come up and both prayers were answered immediately. Normally, such applications take months.

I can't discuss the challenge yet; but it was serious enough for me to do more than pray.

The spiritual strategy I am employing is one that would have me tipped back to the loony unit at prison, if I let on.

It reminds me of my friend Matthew.

He turns six on the 16th or 17th. He is such a strong one. I think it will be a week, before things are back to normal. I think of him rarely; but when I do problems seem to dissolve. It's such a blessing.

Say "hello" to Matthew for me! He loves his tea, coffee, milk and water.

I will write again in about a week.

Love, Trish xx

The preceding letter refers to my intention "to fast" according to Matthew 6:16-17. I didn't want the officers to know.

Journal notes

29th April (Wednesday, 4th day fasting)

The following is based on Matthew 7:6 where Jesus says: "Do not give what is holy to dogs, and do not throw your pearls before swine, or they will trample them under their feet, and turn and tear you to pieces." Remember, in Jewish culture, to call someone a swine was the ultimate insult.

The swine may be my enemy; but is my enemy necessarily a swine?

How do I love my enemy, without casting my pearls? To love is to cast pearls. Or does loving simply mean to serve in silence?

When do I happily risk rejection, and when do I protect myself from being trampled underfoot?

I have become stronger and tougher. My feelings no longer get hurt. Has my heart hardened, or simply matured? Have I lost compassion, or have I recognised when to stop bothering?

I walk a balance beam and try to be as honest as I can with myself and the Lord. I cannot afford to blow the privileged opportunity I have of being in prison.

Like Dostoevsky I say, "There is only one thing I dread: not to be worthy of my sufferings."

In my own words, I say it like this, "Don't stuff up what God is doing, in your life, through this journey!"

It would be easy to come up with a quick, witty answer that eventually becomes a tag-line. For example, "Preach the Gospel, and if necessary, use words."

I think some people use that as an excuse, to avoid the discomfort of acknowledging their faith to someone.

Having chosen not to be ashamed of my faith, and suffered the consequences, I can understand why others are fearful of doing the same.

However, knowing when to speak and, when to be silent, requires depth of thought and true discernment. It requires compassion, an ability to listen and the boldness to actually speak, rather than hide behind simple "niceness."

It seems other people can live the most outrageous lifestyle, believe strange things, and their right to do so is protected; but the Christian cannot.

I am surrounded by profanity and moral bankruptcy, yet I was warned against "*forcing* my beliefs on others!"

Who is warning them not to force their beliefs onto me? I am bombarded by idiotic beliefs.

These are the questions I ponder. I am reluctant to answer myself too quickly. Nor do I want someone else's book or message to tell me. I need to work it out, in my spirit.

15th Letter (unsent)

4th May

I decided not to send this letter, because I didn't want the authorities to know I was fasting. It's supposed to be done in secret, so we can't boast about it. In here, though, it would ring alarm bells. One day of fasting is one thing, but they would not understand me doing it for a week. They already think I am odd.

I have had a victory. I have overcome a major battle. Prayer was not enough to combat the evil. On Saturday 25th as I prayed in the afternoon, I clearly felt God's direction to fast. I had not fasted much in the time leading up to prison. I had not felt strong enough, between the devastation that hit us financially, and the ensuing dramas with ASIC and the legal system.

I wonder now: if I had fasted, would I have broken the ever present pall of depression and anxiety? I used to constantly battle those evil twins with varying degrees of success.

Thank you to those who understood my cryptic message and prayed for me. I have had a better week.

As I began the fast, I knew that it was quite likely I'd be rostered to work in the kitchen, not because I told anyone, but because my resolve would be tested. Irony is a regular part of my life, as you know! When that didn't happen, I knew better than to relax.

I was rostered for the cemetery; but also discovered I was to work Tuesday and Thursday at Meals on Wheels! Then, when a woman injured her finger, I was asked to work there on Wednesday as well. So, during seven days of fasting, I was to spend three of them preparing meals. *Ha!*

Fortunately, by the third day of a fast, you usually are not bothered by hunger pains. "Meals on Wheels" is a nice place to work. A fifteen-minute walk takes us through a familiar neighbourhood I'd worked in, twenty years earlier, as a family portrait photographer. Back then, I certainly hadn't imagined *this* in my future.

Different worlds lay next to one another. "Meals on Wheels" is located right next to the Queensland Cricket Club where I used to attend Women's Network Australia lunches. *I have since resumed my membership and enjoy networking lunches there, again.*

I remember attending one where we brought along business clothes to donate to underprivileged women, so they could go to job interviews well-dressed. Little did I know I would become one of those women!

After my release, I started my own business as a fraud prevention speaker, and the author of "Dangerous Wealth," a book for women on warning signals of fraud and how to bounce back. In 2010, it felt just as strange, to return to lunch with Women's Network Australia, knowing my previous world was still functioning a short distance away. Irony again!

The staff and volunteers at Meals on Wheels were kind and patient. We worked together to prepare meals that are delivered to the elderly or handicapped.

Once the food was cooked, we stood "production-line" style, spooning it into meal trays. Sometimes, soft textures are required; sometimes, it's a special dietary meal.

When completed, we had a break and were invited to serve ourselves, from what was left. Ah, politely declining a baked dinner, or sausages and mashed potato, in favour of a cup of tea, was challenging.

It didn't go unnoticed.

I'm no hero. I know that when we fast, we are not to look like we are denying ourselves, but I could have wept as I watched the last of a scrumptious shepherd's pie being tipped into the rubbish bin!

I watched, fascinated, as the last bit of meat and its glorious juice drizzled down to where its former companions of wasted vegies and other rubbish awaited..!

You can't help but laugh at yourself, in such a situation. Few people understand the strength and reward that comes from denying the flesh. In my case, I didn't want to have to explain myself to the authorities.

On the whole, it was surprisingly easy. Before the seven days were up, I knew something had changed... I had a new strength inside me. It felt like a foundation of stability. On the sixth day, Friday, back at the cemetery, I had been weeding at the cemetery all morning. I prayed through some issues regarding some officers and other prison issues.

Forgiveness was elusive.

I laid bare my underlying anger. I had no substantial answers for myself. I just meditated in the Presence of the Lord; that's at least *something* they couldn't take away from me, as I quietly dug out the weeds.

There was no lightning strike, no clever revelation. I had a desire to forgive; but my feelings were still angry. Then, through nothing I did; but only by His grace, it all lifted off me. I knew the Holy Spirit had done something in me, and I was different.

As it turned out, this was preparation. I fasted for the week, without telling anyone; but it's very hard to hide it. While fasting strengthens you spiritually, it can challenge the current spiritual climate...

I was about to feel the retaliation.

On Saturday, a bossy and controlling woman began to turn her attention to me. Her hair regrowth was the opposite of mine, because it was growing out grey with dark on the ends! She reminded me of a cross-between Cruella de Ville from *"101 Dalmatians,"* and one of those matriarchs from a TV crime family. I tried to be nice; but finally realised a boundary had to be drawn.

It was my job to sweep the floor, after dinner, in the evening. I usually left it until there were fewer people downstairs. This wasn't fast enough for her, and she felt entitled to come and tell me, to go and do it. No doubt she'd spent some time, complaining with her little band of druggie sycophants, about the state of the floor and how slack I was.

She'd said her bit and stalked off. I made a choice. I went and found her. I told her she was not an officer; my chores had nothing to do with her, and while I respected her as a person, she was not to tell me *when and how* I do my chores, or boss me around at all.

I also am learning how to C.Y.A. (It's a business acronym for Cover Your Bottom) I went straight to the officers, to "confess" that I had told someone to mind her own business, and that she might complain about me.

I made a powerful enemy, that night.

Email to readers, from Justin

9th May

(Serious accusation) She needs encouragement.

Hi friends of Trish,

I (Justin) write to you, to bring you up-to-date with a very serious matter concerning Trish. Trish has not asked me to write; but she is in need of as much encouragement as she can get.

Trish has had a rough couple of weeks. Today (Saturday 9th May) on visiting Trish, she told us (her parents, Ian and Jan Ross and me) that, this morning, someone had accused Trish of saying that she wanted to stab someone.

The accuser told the guards that this was what she heard Trish saying. Trish was called into the office and asked if she had said this. Trish said, "No, the accuser is lying." (Trish doesn't know who has made this accusation, and was told, she *won't* be told who it was).

Two of the girls Trish was with, when the accuser had heard this, were called into the office. The two girls who were summoned to the office had no idea why they were being called in, and were asked, "Did Trish say this?"

They both said "No, Trish would never say something like that!"

Trish's main concern is the accuser only needs to "find" one or two of the other girls in there, to "back up her story," to get Trish into serious trouble.

I know that Trish's attitude is to pray for her enemies; not harm them. This is evident in her letters to us.

After discussing with the family what had happened this morning, Trish made a formal complaint to the guards that were on duty, during our visit. I heard Trish say to the guards, she wished to make a formal complaint of the accusation against her, as this was too serious a matter to let slide.

I don't think you, or I, can begin to imagine the mental torture and games that are going on in there. While Trish puts on a brave front and continues the fight, spiritually, I know today she told me that her stomach was churning, feeling "knotted," and she didn't feel safe, and is sick of crying.

She has told the "authorities," she doesn't feel safe.

I wasn't afraid of being harmed physically; however, I was afraid of being set up, and possibly charged with something I didn't do.

Trish has told me that, even trying to keep "a low profile and keep to herself," can get her into trouble for not mixing with the others!

A number of times people have asked me, "If there is anything that we can do, anything, please let us know." (And I do thank you for those kind words of support).

Well, now I would like to ask you all to write an encouraging letter, paragraph or line to Trish, to give her the physical and spiritual lift she needs, in this time. I know a number of you have written a number of times, and continue to keep Trish in your prayers.

I thank you for that, on behalf of Trish and myself. Trish tells me, when she receives mail, how it comes in at the right time and gives her a big "lift." I can always hear it in her voice.

I know the letters, cards and books, people have sent to her; let her know that she is thought of and that you care.

Trish and I both understand that this is a spiritual attack. I know this is our journey; but I also know there is strength in numbers, and that it is easy to be "taken out," going into battle alone.

Thank you for taking the time to write.

Blessings,

Justin Jenkins

Journal notes

13th May

I hate this place.

It feels like a different planet where the expectations of behaviour, right behaviour, is behaviour I would find intolerable in my own world.

Caring about someone is interfering. Defending the weak, exposing a lie, making peace between two people who hate each other, but when each of whom are your friend; all these things are "sin" here. Why? It causes more trouble.

Every woman here has issues of some kind. Normal conversations are not really normal.

When I finally "get it," will it simply mean I have crossed the line and become "institutionalised?"

Journal notes, continued

14th May

"Institutionalised" means you have become so reliant on a system making decisions for you, such as how to behave within the institution, when and what you will eat, who you can see, and monitoring your mail, that you have trouble adapting to the outside world.

For the sake of peace, I must not only try to be invisible; but also be blind and deaf to the needs of others. I must participate in behaviour that I would not tolerate in my own family.

I am a pretty good actor; but in real life I cannot be a fake. Will I be able to "pretend" for the next four months, for the sake of peace? I don't know. I pray for wisdom and I ask if I am a hypocrite? Jail wisdom requires hypocrisy of personal values. Personal values mean less than nothing here, because they can cause conflict.

I'm not referring to expressing views on morality. I refer to being instructed to refrain from simple acts of kindness. Better to be an island.

However, women are relational beings and those who cannot be an island find solace in fitting in with a clique. Unfortunately, these cliques can become "factions" who hate each other. Problems occur, when an "island" befriends people from different "cliques."

How can I be effective in these conditions, when I keep getting into trouble? I got into trouble today, for leaving my radio playing in my room; a breach of the rules. I can pick up the local Christian station.

How do you explain that you do it to keep a clean atmosphere... that to return discouraged, then open the door to anointed music, is a healing balm? How do you explain spiritual warfare, or demonic attacks, without sounding crazy?

I am done with "casting my pearls before swine." It's too hard to tell which ones are swine. I don't care enough, anymore, to put myself "out there." I am trying hard to stay isolated, to spend time reading, writing and in prayer.

Perhaps, I should really throw myself into those things. I could stick to writing out my frustrations, journal and letting the answers come to me. Then maybe I'll be spent, and not have the emotional energy to care about what is happening around me.

I had been kind to a girl, who was being picked on for her crime, when she arrived. Now she has settled in, but sided with those I don't mix with as they don't like me.

...I notice it doesn't hurt.

I don't need those women to like me. I'm grateful that I'm fairly well cured of my "people pleasing" need for approval. However, I don't want to become hardened. I don't want to get to the point where I am desensitised, and have problems, when I leave here.

Holy Spirit, please take over and teach me your ways in this minefield. Help me to stay silent; but not resentful or hostile. I am tempted to harden my heart, and to a degree, I must. Your Word says to ask for wisdom and you will give it. Please give me supernatural wisdom, as "worldly wisdom" is too contradictory and confusing for me. Amen.

I felt a prophetic answer:

"You are a wonderful individual. They are not going to break you! Many people, who are "different," have difficulties conforming: authors, artists, activists, geniuses."

Every person has a calling. Some of them are harmonious, and some are catalysts for change. I won't be taking on the prison system; but I resolve to be an observer, and then ask the Lord for His perspective.

I think I can manage that.

16th Letter

18 May

In eighteen weeks, I walk out of here. Some people have written to say how fast the time has gone. I wish I could say the same. It's true that Friday seems to come around quickly; but individual days seem terribly long. How many more minutes until morning tea? Is it almost lunchtime? Better get ready for the next head count. What will be on TV tonight?

I try to remember to focus on the "Now," to give my attention to the task in front of me. Today, it has been cleaning spectacles. Cleaning involves scrubbing the build-up of a pasty mix of bacteria and D.N.A. Often they are from deceased people. It makes sense that someone, who needed glasses, could not see the grime when they are removed. It can be quite repulsive; but I don't mind. It's temporary.

Are you content in your job? What pressures do you face? Contentment is a learned skill. I have no choice about the jobs I do; but I know they are only temporary, so I don't mind.

Your job is temporary, too.

Are you stuck in a job, while your "vision" remains a hobby? Do you have something great that you want to do for God? Do you imagine that one day you will do it full-time? Maybe you will and maybe you won't. Remember, we discussed praying to *be effective,* rather than praying for provision? Being effective is the priority; don't assume full-time ministry will make you more effective. It won't; but it will narrow your target market.

What a wonderful thing to have a normal job where you can be a light and an influence. How great that it can provide what you need for your vision, in your spare time!

"What spare time?" I hear you ask. Don't get me started on my "Busyness" message. If you are too busy to have a ministry hobby, don't be offended if your market is too "busy" to listen to you!

Get that book written.

Get some part-time training.

Drop unproductive activities.

Make time to relax, because that is productive too.

If you have to work too hard to maintain your lifestyle, sell your big house and get something cheaper. It will take the pressure off.

My needs are very primary. I work full-time. My room and meals are supplied, and I am paid $28.55 per week, plus an amenities allowance of $9.27. I pay $2 a week for TV access. I have to pay for my toiletries, phone calls, and anything else from what's left.

How would you like that budget?

Regards,

Trish

17th Letter

19th May

My dear friends,

You may be aware that I have had a rather eventful past few weeks.

I am OK. I decided to fast from all unnecessary conversation. Alas, I am not very good at it, but I'm getting better.

I was finally sent off for my first mammogram. It didn't take long as there wasn't much to work with!

I spend almost all my spare time, in my room, where I read, write and pray. Sometimes I play cards with a lovely Aboriginal lady of about sixty.

She told me, "I'm learnin' ya how to play 'Two Handed Patience,' orright?"

Orright! I love her to bits. She has an indigenous sixth sense. She finds herself annoyed at someone, without knowing why, and asks me to pray for her attitude. I haven't told her; but a few times I happened to know different ones were criticising her behind her back. She had picked up on it. We call each other "sister-girl;" but sometimes I call her "auntie," out of respect, like the young black girls do; as she is like an aboriginal elder to me when she gives me advice.

You will be pleased to know that my book *"Dangerous Wealth"* is getting a final edit by the lovely Helen. She is hitching up my dangling participles and my publisher will print a run just prior to my release. It's a handbook for women on how to avoid both financial and romantic fraud. "What every women needs to know to avoid being ripped off!"

The book was not published for another year as I was a mess for a while, then rewrote much of it and included that I had been imprisoned. I figured it is best coming from me than people finding out another way.

In the meantime, I'm working on my second book which will be in diary format, including some of my emails, and the details I've not been able to share yet. Hopefully, there will be enough hard won wisdom in it to make it worthwhile; written in the midst of the battle and all that...

Thank you so much, to those of you who wrote to me. I really needed that and I read your letters over and over. They are like fresh air to me.

Take care, my friends; and be sure to care about one another.

Love, Trish

Journal notes

20th May

I am remaining quiet; a recluse for now. In a few weeks, the tone will change and hostilities will shift. Sometimes the change in tone is swifter. The best advice I received, came from a friend of a friend who had done time. I must try to be invisible, just observe and try to pick up on the mood of the day.

Yesterday, the mood was hostile and resentful. It was raining so hard the women, who normally worked at the cemetery, had to stay in. We would have extra people working at grading glasses with me.

Noting who they were, I quietly suggested to the officers that since there were so many of us, perhaps I could do some jobs that don't normally get done. It made sense, and I spent the morning cleaning out the kitchen pantry and shelves.

Then the power went out, in the rear building, where the glasses were done, so all the equipment was brought up to the dining room. Several times I had to pass through them, to retrieve or empty a mop bucket and I could sense their hostility. "Why aren't you working with us? We are short of people!"

"You have the cemetery girls working here, so I'm doing stuff that otherwise doesn't get done." I answered and kept going. People get disturbed, when someone is doing something different. They suspect they are missing out or the person has an unfair advantage.

The tone is horrible and I'd just like to avoid them, until it passes. It's ironic that we are to mind our own business; but members of a group have a deep interest in anything one person does that stands out.

Bitchy and critical talk is the order of the day. For example, in the afternoon I was back doing glasses. One cemetery girl kept making comments on how little had been achieved, since the last delivery. I ignored her and wondered why it mattered anyway.

Fortunately, it gave me time to think and I finally said, "They arrived late Friday, I washed them all day yesterday, and the two girls with me were brand new. They actually did a really good job, for new people. Accuracy is more important than speed."

I would have said nothing; except that one of those new girls was with us and I didn't want her to get discouraged.

Silly me, I should have said nothing. Some people think that to disagree is to insult them.

In a place where kindness is considered weakness, it follows that knowing *that*, but to choose kindness anyway, is very courageous.

It can also be foolish; as it can be easily twisted. It has been very hard for me to put away my instinct for encouragement. I also have come to see, I make a habit of excusing the poor behaviour of others. I believe I do this in order to avoid seeing the bad side of a person.

More accurately, I can avoid accepting they just plain dislike me. My past need for acceptance meant I would gloss over signs of rejection, because to recognise it would be painful.

The mature step, of course, is to accept the behaviour was bad. They don't like me; they do reject me; but that is their problem, not mine. If there is something I have done to cause it, then I can accept that, apologise and move on. If not, I can move on anyway.

How free it is not to be captive to the approval of others. Sure, in some contexts of life, approval is necessary; however, just as we are encouraged to "do our own time," we must also "live our own lives." Comparing your skills or material success to others is not helpful.

You are responsible for the life you've been given.

I am currently reading Victor Frankl's book, *"Man's Search for Meaning."* He was a psychologist and a Holocaust survivor. In his book, he challenges the common question of, "What can I get out of life?"

He suggests that in fact, life asks us, "What are you contributing to Life?"

What are you doing that matters?

We had three new receptions today. A young girl sat beside me at lunch, and I tried hard not to make unnecessary conversation. I answered her questions briefly and kept to myself. I felt frustration building, as I cannot accept that contradictory rules are justified. While I shall remain quiet, kindness must carry an acceptable risk.

While I won't interfere in someone else's dispute, how can I be like the Levi and priest who walked past a wounded man? The Samaritan didn't, and the rules of society said he should have.

> "Do not withhold what is good from those to whom it is due when it is in your power to give it."
>
> (Proverbs 3:27)

Finally, I looked at the girl and smiled. I spoke softly and asked, "Would you like some unsolicited advice?"

"Yes, please."

"Don't get caught up in the gossip and bitchiness. Anything you do will be talked about and the littlest thing you do will be reported by a tattle-tale. Other than that, you'll be fine."

"Thank you so much." She was relieved and smiled; not just because she had been given a tip, but because someone cared enough to bother with her.

What an upside down world this is.

Journal notes, which evolved into a letter I decided not to post.

21st May

HALFWAY POINT!

Whenever my name is called my stomach turns. You never know if there is something you have done, or someone has reported you for something, even by making it up.

Yesterday, it was simply that I had forgotten to add HJC (Helena Jones Centre) to the return address on my mail out. I wasn't in trouble. The day before, I was called in response to a query I had made. I was hoping I wasn't in trouble for that and I wasn't.

Even at the 6.30 head count this morning, my friend stood next to me, half-asleep. I naturally put my arm around her back. An officer asked me if she were OK, and I said, "She's just sleepy."

"You are comforting her?" She said, in an accusing tone. I shrugged and dropped my arm. My friend was called over and I wondered if I had done something wrong, my stomach turning again.

Fortunately, it was about her mail and had nothing to do with me.

I marvelled at my paranoia.

It's not unfounded paranoia, however, as I must be ever on guard. We are, after all, constantly treated with suspicion.

I cannot prove anything; but it would not surprise me, if a recent accusation made against me was a fiction made up by a particular person, I had told not to boss me around.

We are now not permitted to speak to one another or even be in a room together. If they really thought I was a threat, I would have been tipped-back to the prison immediately.

It's totally against my faith to accept not speaking to someone, but I didn't have the mental or emotional strength to make the argument.

For now, I practice being invisible and speaking only when necessary.

Today marks the halfway point of my sentence. This year may have flown for you; but it has dragged for me. I am told by other prisoners that the second half will go faster. It's a downhill run. I hope so.

I feel like a caterpillar hiding in a chrysalis. The Lord is doing a deep work in me to answer my prayer that I be "effective"... And whatever else He wants.

Don't worry; I'm sure I won't be too "weird," like those people who go on mission trips to a Third World country; but return angry, and hating the rest of us spoiled, rich Westerners.

I love you spoiled, rich Westerners! I am spoiled and rich, too; compared to Third World people.

Ah, if it weren't for a sense of humour, I would have despaired and given in to depression. No amount of anti-depressants can lift what incarceration does to the soul. I know that first hand.

The authorities wanted me to stay on anti-depressant, anti-anxiety pills, until after I leave. Then it will be my family dealing with me coming off them. *Ha! No way!*

I decided to get off them while I'm here under their supervision, so I can be totally free well before reuniting with my family. They have suffered enough without having to deal with that. I had taken them in the lead-up to court, because it was all just too much for me.

The last thing I wanted was to expose my children to my inner terror.

You can judge me for not having enough faith, but I won't judge you for your imperfections. I did what I needed to, in order to function for my family. I wasn't as strong then, as I am now.

Sure, I have anxious moments now; but I am not depressed. I face each of my "demons" as they turn up. The Lord shows me how to deal with them. It's like therapy on my own, in my room.

I am not afraid.

Take care of each other. At the end of the day, that is all that matters.

Love, Trish xxxx

Terror in the office!

I was rostered for a week to do the nightly clean of the reception and office domain. It is a high security area. I'm only required to wipe bench tops, empty the bins, clean their bathroom and floors. The bins overflow with shredded files, the secret information they have on us.

A camera watches my every move; but, even so, why any prisoner is trusted in there alone with other people's sensitive information; I don't know!

I was nervous. My nerves were already shot, and I didn't want to be any closer to officers and officialdom than absolutely necessary. I also wanted to do a good job, so they wouldn't have reason to criticise me.

The reception area was filthy. Dust caked the window sills, wall switches, computer tops and, gathered at the rear of benches, where computer cords snaked and tangled together.

I decided to run a rag over some of these areas to dust them. As I wiped the top of a little box protruding from the wall, the curved knuckle of my middle finger brushed the button on the face of the box.

Suddenly, the fluorescent light went out and instead, a blue light flashed round and round the room. At the same time, an ear-splitting "Whoop! Whoop!" sounded repeatedly!

I froze in terror; arms out, dust cloth in one hand, fully expecting the uniforms to burst in and throw me on the floor!

Well, two officers came in, turned the light on and ignored me. "Where is the damn switch to turn this off?" One yelled to the other.

"Is that it? I'm sorry, I was dusting that box." I pointed, trembling, to the switch.

"No, Jenkins; that is the alarm! Don't touch it."

Still the "Whoop, Whoop!" continued.

I started to see how funny we looked and bit my lip.

Eventually they found the kill switch. I was warned not to touch anything electrical, next time, and told to leave.

Phew!

Journal notes

1st June

I don't want "Break-Even."

I want "Break-Through!"

Peace is not enough.

I want to take ground.

Fasting again today. Once again the gentle fire is being fanned and is flaring up.

The worst is behind me. *Or so I thought.*

I believe I broke the Jezebel spirit's power over my life here. It still lurks around; but is not as strong as it was. Two friends went home this morning. One I have known since S9. She has been a great friend. I am happy for her; but I am tearful at losing her.

Kelly is still a precious friend. She had been a Christian growing up; but drifted away from her faith when she went from a Christian school to a rough state school. She says her faith has been revived, by our friendship.

Kelly wrote a poem for me, after she got out, and gave me permission to share it with you:

An innocence about u is lost,
Ur living in the darkest place of all.
How can u ever b the same again? You've hit rock bottom,
What a bloody long way to fall.

So they say u r here to b corrected
Not as punishment for yr crime
But we have all been badly affected
By this criminal production line

Things that u see, I can't even begin…

There is no escape from the misery u feel
When loved ones come to visit
u tell them yr ok
n put on a fake smile.

Never in a million yrs
Would u really tell them what goes on or how u feel
U keep that all inside
to protect them from feeling the way u do

Release day is near, but u await it with fear
As I walk out the gate,
I can't help but look back at this amazing girl still there…
I can't believe I'm leaving without my best mate.

Since I've been out I try to block
These memories from my mind
But when I least expect it
They creep up from behind.

The end of our journey in hell
That will forever encase our heart
Our sentence is for life
People tend to forget that part

I still haven't recovered n don't think I ever will
One of my favourite girls is still on the inside
I will b there till she is out
My friendship will never waiver, of that I have no doubt.

So I sit here n wonder how it is possible to feel
Worse now than I ever did when I was inside n
Then I realise it's because
I had you by my side.

So I say thank u, good luck n goodbye.

I missed her terribly. Fortunately, we stayed friends and still keep in touch today.

18th Letter

2nd June

Hello Friends and Family,

Is it really June at last? Back in January, June seemed a life-time away. It has felt like a life time, too!

I'm not quite ready to write to you about the events of the last six to eight weeks.

If I thought I had fought lions and bears before, the challenges I have overcome lately were even greater. I have become like an undercover commando.

So here's some of what went on:

I did a lot of fasting. I lost 4kg (8.8lbs) in less than a week. It's hard to fast, in a place like this, where meals are allocated. I tried to keep it secret; but some of the women gossiped about me having bulimia!

One week we were out doing a course. After lunch, I went to the bathroom and a nasty girl told everyone I was throwing up! They were very bitchy, in the afternoon. It was like being bullied by badly behaved schoolgirls.

I already mentioned not going to Warwick anymore. I didn't mind. Some people are best avoided.

It was back to the cemetery then. I like it there. However, there was an incident that I still find hilarious...but nobody else does.

We were being allocated areas to weed. I looked at the map which was colour-coded. The supervisor pointed to a coloured patch for two of us to work at. It was the North-West corner. I figured I'd just keep walking till I hit the last bay of tombstones and work backwards. No problem.

What I hadn't noticed was a detail on the map (further out) that wasn't coloured. Two of us headed past the allocated patch, to the furthest corner. We chatted away as we worked, unmindful of what was going on back at the shed...

At one point, we saw a police car zoom past on the road beside us. We joked about who they might be chasing! At five minutes to morning-tea time, we got up, stretched and headed back to the shed.

As we approached, an officer from the Centre was walking rapidly up the hill towards us. It wasn't unusual, because they often did spot checks. He was a nice man, and one of us joked, "Has someone gone missing?"

"Yes. YOU!" We laughed, thinking he was joining in.

But he wasn't smiling.

"Peter (the supervisor) knew where we were. He sent us to the far corner to weed." We explained.

"He reported you missing; so I've come down. The police are out looking for you!"

"You can't be serious? That's ridiculous!" I exclaimed.

Typical, naïve me. It wasn't ridiculous. It was serious. We wouldn't have been the first to just wander away from the low security activities.

The supervisor normally drives up and down the driveways between the sections of graves, checking on us every so many minutes. Since we had gone further than we were supposed to, he couldn't see us.

I often forget that I am among criminals, so I also often forget how serious the protocols are. This poor man had to report us missing, alert police, explain to his boss why we had gone missing on his watch and who knows what else? He was stressed and very cross. No doubt, he would be in trouble, for not finding us.

He said angrily, "I drove up every driveway looking for you and you weren't there!"

To me, it was simple. I looked at the map again, and said, "There we were, right at the corner."

"No, that is the corner. You were past where I said to go."

"Oh. Oops!"

"Oops" didn't help in my ASIC interview and it didn't help me now. This time, though, I could see the funny side of the fuss created and I tried to make light of it. It was so bizarre that I couldn't stop laughing.

My companion's reasonable observation didn't help. "You couldn't have driven up every road or you would have seen us. We would have waved, like we normally do!" It was true; but better left unsaid.

That did it! We were well and truly put in our places, with both profanity and volume. I'm sure the Vatican heard it.

Sadly, my companion was very upset by the ordeal. She was so angry with me, for dropping us in the proverbial "poo," then laughing about it, that she stopped talking to me. Immediately, she was surrounded by sympathetic females, who love a drama and an excuse to bitch about a person - me this time.

Two days, later, I was off the cemetery team.

Officially, it had nothing to do with the incident. I had lost so much weight that my jeans kept slipping and I asked Peter for a piece of rope to use as a belt.

He reported that I flirted with him. Don't think so! He also complained that I preferred to sit with the staff than the other prisoners; which was actually true.

We were allowed to sit with the staff. Normally, we all did; but these girls had to go outside to smoke and they were not friends of mine anyway. Why would I go outside with them, while they smoked; when I could sit at the table and eat my lunch like a normal person?

I must admit, I did find hanging out with blokes refreshing for a change; but I guess I invaded their masculine space. I'm not good at taking hints, so that is understandable...

I was grounded.

I was back to grading second-hand spectacles for the Lion's Club and training people in that process. I quite liked that work. I got to know the new ones coming through and it was a worthwhile project.

I tried to stick to myself, as much as possible. Fasting provides great clarity. I knew I was under spiritual attack. There were new people around. There always are; but each batch brings a different attitude and atmosphere with them.)

18th *Letter, continued*

At one stage, my goal was just to get through without getting into more trouble and, without being a target for someone else's nastiness.

I knew it wouldn't last. You can't escape your training, and I am a warrior. I'm not satisfied with passivity, self-preservation and selfishness.

I had resolved not to speak unnecessarily, and that was a good thing, to a degree. We are all expected to mind our own business in here. That includes not caring about others. I was told by an officer that unless someone specifically says, "Trish, please encourage me," I must ignore them. So I kept to myself.

I ignore the new people, as they come through. I did not volunteer any of my skills, when a project came up, even when I had talent for it. Apart from basic courtesy, something required by "The Rules," I squashed every natural impulse and gift inside me.

I became aware that I was behaving like Christians, who go to church on Sunday, but outside those hours they are no different to the world. Not overtly sinning; but not caring enough to enter the discomfort and joy of making a connection with their neighbour. The excuse may be that they are "too busy;" but don't get me started on that topic…

I began to feel a righteous rebellion rising. You see, I still spend time in prayer, time in the word and spiritual strategies (*fasting*). Then I had a revelation that I began to meditate on. It's quite a significant thing in a dark place like this:

In a place where kindness is considered weakness, to be aware of that, to know that everyone is aware of that, and to choose to be kind anyway - that is extremely courageous!

One night, another "newbie" sat next to me. She had a fresh young face, never been in trouble before. I tried to ignore her. I answered her questions, in monosyllables.

She was so vulnerable, scared. I'm sure it was the Holy Spirit, rising up in me, prompting the thought, "Blow it!"

I turned to her and said, "Come and I'll show you where to clean your plate." She followed and I gave her some tips on coping in here. She was so relieved and grateful, "Thank you" she gasped. Further details (following that story) will be available after I leave here. Suffice to say she is learning how to be content while awaiting a miracle.

(*This girl has since asked Jesus into her life*).

The abovementioned girl had lost her driver's licence, due to accumulating demerit points. She had left her car in her work car park. Police saw her car, at her work and concluded she had been driving it unlicensed!

They arrested her on the spot, in front of her colleagues, and took her off to the watch-house. Weeks later, from prison, she was still trying to prove she hadn't driven her car, and now had us as housemates! I prayed with her regularly.

She was successful in her case and was released. However, who knows what affect her ordeal had on her life?

You can't un-ring that bell.

By the way, "thank you" to the friends who wrote me, to ensure I didn't get proud about my "no unnecessary talking" effort. Apparently, it struck some of you as hilarious, if not impossible; not to mention how *good* it would be for me - thanks!

I issue a challenge right back at you. Fast from unnecessary talk for even a day. Let me know how you get on. I promise I won't make fun of how badly you need to do it.

"Jezebel" has been bound; but regularly attempts to rear up. I remain on guard, ready to smash her down, as needed. It takes less effort these days.

I know my authority and where the battle really is:

Ephesians 6 and Matthew 6 are commando verses.

People can't tell what I am doing or why; but things change.

Take care, all.

God bless,

Trish

Journal notes

5th June

I had a bit of fun with a young woman who is in for cooking up her own drugs. She lives across the hall, a big, cheerful girl. She asked me if I had any treats. I gave her the remainder of a box of TV snacks I could do without. She insisted I take her packet of "orange rollers," in return. They are the generic brand of "Jaffas," chocolate balls covered in a hard orange shell.

Back in my room, I ate a few, then a few more. I realised that even though I wasn't enjoying them, I was eating them, because they were there. No way! I took them back and said, "I can't keep these; if I do I'll eat the lot and be sick. You have them."

"I'll keep them for you for tomorrow," she suggested.

"No thanks."

"Really, you might want them…"

"That's why I have to have them out of my room altogether!"

As I walked away I turned, raised my hand as though dangling temptation, and did my best impression of a drug pusher, "C'mon, I know you want them, when you do, I'll be right here…you can't stay away from it…you'll…be…back…mwah ha ha ha" (sinister laugh).

"Is that a good impression of a drug pusher?" I asked her.

She laughed, "Yep!"

I left and then flung her door open again for my best Devil/Count Dracula laugh, "Mwah ha ha ha!"

She was fun and very intelligent. I found her refreshing.

I asked her about her profession, and how it compared to the movies and documentaries I'd seen. She was very matter of fact about it all. "Well, they don't show you what really happens; because they can't help people work it out. It takes the right ingredients at the right time…

"So... you're a chef then!"

She thought that was very funny. She is a bright, popular girl. No one would pick her for a criminal, let alone a drug producer. It was only when we talked about other things that her godless perspective showed itself. I've never heard someone so jaded, with almost no sense of right and wrong, and yet so charming.

19th Letter (Unsent)

Sometime in June

Prayer Request

Hello All,

I am currently praying for a matter that is disturbing about half a dozen ladies. We are in a quandary, and the question is:

"Does the squeaky wheel really get the oil, or does it just push your application further to the bottom of the 'in-tray'?"

The result is that the women are afraid to "squeak;" but are becoming upset and angry. For some time, we accept the excuse, "Oh, it's just been so busy..."

There is that word "Busy," again. *As my friend Kelly said, "We are their job! This is what they are supposed to be doing; they should not be too busy to do it!"*

We know things that are supposed to happen take time, that there are delays, so we try not to get our hopes up. Then, after a time, we look up and realise something is genuinely amiss.

The issue is this:

When someone has been at Helena Jones Centre for one month, they can apply for "Re-Integration Leave." It's a twelve-hour pass to go home to see our families.

Once the application is in, the parole board takes twenty-eight days (give or take) to do a home inspection, to make sure you will not be at risk of drugs, weapons or criminal elements. A report is drafted and returned to HJC after another week (or two).

Then a designated person here takes a week to write a report on you. Then there is the same to-ing and fro-ing for approvals and signatures from various authorities.

Then you apply for a particular day and that can take a week for approval.

If all had gone according to the expected time frames, even allowing for the longer times, I would have had a home visit back in MAY!

It occurred to me that NOBODY has had a first home visit, since I have been here. Suddenly, there is a group of us waiting expectantly. One lady started the process back in February. *Someone wasn't doing their job and it was affecting lives! Even as I type this out, more than a year later, I feel the same outrage building up. I had forgotten this story.*

We put on a smile, as we gently query what stage the process is up to. We hide our frustration and dismay, in order to avoid the humiliation of being told off for "acting above ourselves... telling them their job... it's a privilege, not a right... blah, blah, blah."

"Re-Integration Leave" is provided to help us adjust to life outside prison, in a safe environment. It's very restricted; no stopping on the way home, ring as soon as you get there and an officer may drop in, unannounced, to make sure you have not left the house. Plus, there are random phone calls to check up on us. All this is fair enough. It will be worth it.

All these delays serve to remind me just how low our status is. We are Matthew 26:45. We are the least in society.

Last night, I became quite angry as my "fix-it" nature rose up. I had an 'imaginary conversation' that, even in my imagination, did not end well!

I then chose the better strategy which is to pray and fast. *My prayer and fasting did work; but not for me!*

Please pray for peace and harmony here. When the ladies are distressed they take it out on each other. Please also pray that our applications move along quickly, as it is a precious thing to us.

Even writing this letter is a risk.

Love, Trish

20th Letter (Unsent)

Still June

Dear All,

I am living a testimony that I know I will share with the Body of Christ later. I am conscious of wanting it to be successful.

How would we deal with challenges, if we knew that one day we would be telling the story from a platform? What plans of action would we report, we had put into place? How did we pull ourselves out of the pits of discouragement?

Why not write your testimony so far? What will you preach, regarding your prayer life, your personal disciplines, your revelations, received as you pressed into God?

Are you already thinking of how you can help others?

You may not preach; but one day you *will* share your story with others. Will it be a story explaining or excusing your broken, defeated life, or will it be a story that glorifies God, because you overcame?

The good news is your story is not over. If you are defeated, you can still rise again. Don't give up, just change your expectations. See where you need to change yourself and your previous assumptions.

How do you face trouble? Psalm 91 is a key:

> ¹⁴ "Because he has set his love upon Me, therefore I will deliver him;
> I will set him on high, because he has known My name."

What is your part in God's deliverance? In order to hide in the Lord, you must love Him. To love Him you need to know Him.

To love the Lord without reverence is a shallow, conditional love. When things get tough, many people begin by demanding the Lord fix their problems. When it doesn't look like God is working for them *(note, "for them")*, their love turns cold and, like a fickle lover, they desert Him.

Spiritual maturity is to grow from infatuation to surrender, trust and friendship.

How do you face trouble? According to verse 14 of Psalm 91, you set your love upon Him and you know His name.

"Setting your love" indicates a conscious choice.

"Know His Name" means understanding who He is.

Ephesians 6 talks about the armour of God. We have spiritual warfare to do, sure, but finally, "having done all....stand."

I face my battles this way: I think of them, I stand, close my eyes, draw a breath, square my shoulders, and exhale slowly. In that breath, I consciously place myself in His hands. I am resolute in going through whatever will happen.

Am I scared? Sure, but it's like I am watching it happen around me, knowing God is invisibly at work. I can get through it.

Whatever your battle is, have God as your ally. If you feel like He's not doing His part, it's your perception that needs to change. Be open minded enough to consider you may not have the right perspective. Job never cursed God and after his troubles, he was blessed way beyond what he had before. He also lived another 140 years!

Job was a radical thinker, for his time. In chapter 42:15 it says his daughters received *their own inheritance* among their brothers.

I don't believe he only did that because he was so wealthy he could afford to let it overflow. He was wealthy, but he was his own man. He saw no need to comply with society's expectations. If he had, he would have listened to his friends and failed.

I reckon Job would have been a fantastic Dad to those girls. Now there is a study!

Like Job, walk your own path; but trust in God. Sometimes all that is left is to "stand."

21st Letter

20th June

Hello all,

I had a wonderful visit from friends who were up from New South Wales. As soon as they heard I'd "gone away," they filled out a "Form 27" to come and visit me. It was quite touching to know that, way back in January, they planned their anniversary holiday to include visiting me.

Seeing people from outside my family circle reminds me that the world is still turning, out there, and it won't be long before I join you.

The thought of attending the Christian Outreach Centre national conference is a little daunting, but I have enough friends to be able to ignore any nasty whispers.

Maybe I should get that prison tattoo, to really give them something to talk about???

God is so good. He uses the most unlikely people to show us ourselves. Lately, I've noticed several girls say to me "Trish, don't make excuses for her!" Where there is bad behaviour, I often quietly say, "She's just doing that because she's this or that." It's my way of keeping the peace and staying quiet.

It was after this that I realised I did this to avoid facing unpleasantness and rejection.

A special "hello" to Ps Jeanette Smith and family. You already have my private letter; but I would like once again to honour Ps John Smith who passed away recently. John introduced me to a living Christ who is real and relevant in our lives today; someone who is more than a historical figure, someone who works miracles still.

John truly was a great man of God. If more pastors were like him, the Church would have fewer "spots and wrinkles," bless her heart.

21ˢᵗ Letter continued

21ᵗʰ June

God is so good! I have suffered massive persecution, in the last few weeks. There have been a lot of dramas, among the girls, this week; over all sorts of things.

Tonight, it was all worth it. I can't go into detail; but I had an amazing victory that makes all the bulldust worth it. The thing about our challenges is that they drive us into the Presence of God. I've been angry and frustrated, many times this week.

I said to the Lord, "If I'm not going to take any more ground, what is the point in me being here? Is it to teach me patience? OK. I'm not allowed to talk about you or offer to pray for anyone. Even the chaplains caution me to say nothing."

Some of you beloved friends have also cautioned me to just look out for me. Well, I stay quiet, yet watchful. I pray, I ask the Lord to encourage me with His Perspective. I've asked Him, "Will there be any more? Yes, there are more.

I don't know who they are; but tonight there is a party going on in Heaven. The anointing was so strong, I almost felt drunk. Any discomforts and nasty injustices lost all power by comparison to the joy that filled me and "others."

I felt a new strength flow through me. I was conscious of a new anointing, hard to describe. It's quieter, yet powerful. I am limited as to the detail I can write, but those among you who move in the gifts of the Spirit will understand.

I was able to minister to some women who had massive breakthroughs. One had been in a COC church as a youth; but gone off the rails and now felt like she couldn't come back. That is all changed. Every bit of nastiness was worth suffering to see the joy and peace that shone from her face.

The word "subversive" has been floating around, in my mind, all week. I recall a prophecy I received many years ago that I would be a "designated hitter." If I quietly make a strategic strike, here and there, it is just as effective as an alter call.

It's not about me being clever, far from it. It's a privilege to be in my position. I will be able to share more exciting details, when I am released.

In the meantime, please pray for me to be effective and pleasing to those who, like Nebuchadnezzar, have authority over my daily activities; but do not understand the authority they are under.

I never imagined quite so much ground could be taken by me being in here. Is being in here worth it? I never would have seriously thought so; but it is. Still, I'm not satisfied.

The final three months will not be wasted; softly, softly...

Bless you heaps,

Take courage!

Trish.

As I read over this last letter, I am not surprised that they were on the lookout for an excuse to get rid of me... and it wasn't long before I gave them one.

TIPPED BACK!

22nd Letter

7th July

Hi friends,

Well, another adventure has begun. After my last big victory, I felt that all the challenges and setbacks had been worth it. There were only twelve weeks to go, how bad could it get?

Another part of my brain reminded me that dynamics change from week to week. A lot can happen in a short space of time. "Don't get complacent."

On Friday 26 June, in the late afternoon, I got "tipped back" to BWCC. I'm not complaining, as it was a "fair cop." A young woman with pre-teen maturity had been annoying all of us with her rudeness and aggression for several weeks.

I had tried to be kind, understanding and patient. I tried to explain that it's better to be respectful of a person than being a smart-Alec.

Then I gave up, as I am not her mother and it was not my place to correct her. However, I am also not a tattle-tale, so I would not complain to the officers. On the outside I wouldn't hesitate to call crime-stoppers; but jail is jail. We're already here. Dobbing doesn't help.

This young woman got away with things that would have tipped others back to the prison. *For some reason, she was able to get away with breaking rules that would get the rest of us tipped-back. These breaches included; but are not limited to: not showing up for head-count, not returning to work on time after a break, refusing to work, swearing at officers, eating all the left-over food and desserts and generally causing strife. I later heard she had friends tossing drugs over the fence for her; but who knows?*

Then it occurred to me that she may have been so annoying, back in the prison, that she was better protected at HJC.

Well, I lost patience and, fed up with her rudeness, I deliberately did something I shouldn't have. Better Christians than me would have lasted longer. I quietly spoke in "tongues," knowing she would freak out - and she did. It was manipulative and a misuse of the gift, but a part of me enjoyed it.

Then I carelessly turned it into a funny story for you. *Not cool.*

I got "tipped" for deliberately provoking someone to freak out. It was a "fair cop."

The good news is I really needed a break from Helena Jones, for reasons I can't go into. I am in S1 (where the bad girls go), where we spend a lot of time locked in our cells.

It has been very restful.

The story so far: A truck, similar to the one that brought me to prison, picked me up and returned me to BWCC via the Princess Alexandra hospital, where we picked up two men returning to prison. I chatted with one through the wall. He has served seven and a half years, so far of a ten to twelve year sentence for murder. Apparently, he'd shot his wife's lover. He was very encouraging, reminding me that twelve weeks will go very quickly. In his world, it's a very short stretch.

I arrived at BWCC reception, handed over my belongings, and was issued with a new uniform, a bar of soap, and toothpaste. I didn't get a phone call, as I was not "new." It was after 5 p.m. on Friday afternoon and they wanted to go home. I heard talk about overtime only being paid for one hour.

At least, they get to go home.

At reception, I was informed that I was going to S1. I only wanted to know if I would be physically safe there. Once assured that I would be, I was calm and confident again. I knew there was a good chance I'd know people there already.

It was too late for me to be given any dinner. Fortunately, I was fasting again anyway. My fast was to strengthen my prayers for our "home day-visits" to be expedited.

I wasn't going to get that approval now!

S1 is a series of buildings surrounding an officer's "fishbowl" and connected by cages. Each building is called a unit, each unit has two pods. Each pod contains a room with six cells coming off it.

One of the buildings is called S4. That is where the mentally affected people go and those who have tried to kill themselves. They appear to be kept on heavy drugs and walk past our cage like zombies under escort.

I was very distraught at my family not knowing where I was and that Justin would be heading off to visit me on Saturday. I kept asking officers, if they could let him know I wasn't there, as I knew HJC would not bother.

No one was interested.

It took a while for me to get past intense anger at the Helena Jones supervisor and staff. Not for tipping me; but for deliberately not informing my family of my move, knowing they were booked in to visit the next day. They cited "privacy reasons." Rubbish. It was a rude, cruel and spiteful act.

Finally, after 11a.m. on Saturday, an officer at BWCC took pity on me and rang Justin's mobile. He had already left, of course, but pulled over to take the call. I knew the news would be devastating for my family; but there was nothing I could do except pray.

As expected, Helena Jones Centre had not bothered to notify expected visitors. It was a lucky coincidence that my children were not coming that day. They would have been crushed. I wonder how the staff would have handled it, if Justin had arrived and made a scene. He was really angry.

Each time I thought of my family, I would work to fight tears of despair. I didn't win every fight. At one stage, I was so upset I had to run and throw up!

I have to say, the women in here with me are just beautiful. Their acceptance is probably more due to my being recognised by one of them. "Trish, what the #$%*? What the #$%&* are you doing in here?"

"I was bad," I said sheepishly. I was relieved to see her lovely, familiar face. She accepted me, so they accepted me. It was like balm to my raw nerves.

Even though they are considered among the worst, these women are not nasty like some of the ones I had been living with. Perhaps, they don't feel the need to "prove" themselves? Perhaps, they can see, I am so different from them that I am not a threat to their world? I'm a bit of a novelty. Certainly they can't understand how a "straighty" like me ended up there! My response is to insist, "Hey, I did something really bad, so they sent me here with you toughies. They must think I'm a "toughie" too!"

That makes them laugh.

Because of the rush in processing me, some of the personal items I required were overlooked. These girls were very generous with personal items. I have had to wait for things such as shampoo. When one discovered, I was using margarine to stop my lips drying out, she gave me some of her moisturiser.

I hadn't been issued any sneakers or socks, either. The middle of winter and I'm wearing flip-flops. It was so cold; I wrapped a towel around my feet at night.

The myth of "Duty of Care" is evident by the "not my job" attitude of the staff. No one was working in Reception, on the weekend, so nothing could be done. I was told on Monday to put a request form in and wait for it to be processed...

To be fair, on Monday, the same officer, who had called Justin for me, could see I was freezing, "Why are you wearing thongs (flip flops)?" He personally saw that I was able to get some necessary items.

If prisons employed more caring people like this man, they would find much more cooperative inmates, and the rehabilitation programs would be more effective.

My phone finally got hooked up on Wednesday, so I had the emotional connection with my family. It's a communal phone shared between eleven of us and, each call cuts out, after ten minutes. S1 is the unit they threaten you with, if you misbehave. S4 is part of it and is for the mentally unstable.

The only worse place is the D.U. or Detention Unit. I've written about it before. It's for people caught with drugs or who assault someone, serious breaches like these.

Our pod has a kitchenette and a dining table with stools attached. Both pods open to a shared concrete cage, which is an outside area. It is where we use the telephone. In S1 my unit is Unit 5, my pod is 5A and my cell is Cell 1. It's an "Observation cell." That means there is a camera watching me do *everything*. Fortunately, there is no risk of me doing anything bad and I am mentally strong with no thought of self-harm.

I can't help but wonder what kind of people watch us for the wrong reasons...

Sometimes, I can turn off my own light, and sometimes they have to do it from the fishbowl. Sometimes, the officer on duty cannot find the switch and, of course, that is somehow my fault. One night, I had to sleep with the light on all night.

One refused to turn the light off, because I was in the "Observation" cell and he insisted it needed to stay on. A different officer informed me that I wasn't actually being "observed."

Then there was the night the plumbing kept making a loud sucking noise like the sound made at the last few seconds of draining a bath. I put a towel over the shower drain and in the sink, to muffle it. There was nothing the officers could do about it.

The inconsistencies were frustrating as it became clear each staff member had different training or there is a lack in the "Policy and Procedures" manual. They lock us in our cells for half-a-day every Wednesday afternoon, while they have "Professional Development Training."

Hmmm.

Officers are surprisingly well-mannered with the women in S1. It might be because these women can be particularly volatile, so it would be foolish to antagonise them.

The prayer that bounces me back most quickly is, "Give me Your perspective on this." Even though I put myself here, His hand is in it.

The hardest thing was letting go of feeling responsible for my family's reaction. As usual, my amazing family rose to the occasion. Even though being sent back here is supposed to be a "bad" thing, there are so many things I am grateful for:

1. I landed in a unit with a great bunch of girls, one I was already friends with, and I knew half the others.

2. The gym. I've been there twice and I'm running again. The first time, I just ran and ran and ran around the court. I can tell I'm much fitter than I was before. At one stage, I was 65kg, now I'm 57kg.

Losing 8kg (17.6lbs) isn't much, but it's more than 10% of me.

It was cold and I ran barefoot around the concrete floor; but I didn't care. It was so good to stretch out. It felt therapeutic. I had been given my flip flops; but my sneakers were still with my property at Reception.

It's the middle of winter. They don't care that I only had flip-flops for my feet and I couldn't run in those.

I just had to run.

Some dark girls were watching me run. "Hey you! Come here!" I stopped and went over. I didn't know if they would be friend or foe, so I got in first. I asked them if they knew an Aboriginal

217

friend I had helped write a parole application. "Yes I know her on the outside. She's my cousin," said a big girl. Many of them are cousins.

"Will you say 'hello' to her for me? She'll remember me as the one who used to pray for her."

They all looked at me, and one asked, "Do you do that 'tongue' thing?" *Uh oh, here we go.*

"Er... yes; but it kinda gets me in trouble."

We had a great chat about why I was tipped. "I used my gift for bad instead of good," I said. They laughed, "Nobody's perfect! That's why we're in jail!"

Yep, I really like the Indigenous women.

Interestingly, my reason for getting tipped has resulted in some great conversations about God's love (and how I hadn't always used it!).

Still I was concerned, when they asked me to explain and demonstrate my prayer language. I made a reluctant show of not wanting to freak them out. That made them more interested, of course. I did pray for someone with a particular problem and the problem went away.

Over the time, I've prayed for three people to get parole and they did. Unfortunately, I met two of them again when I was "tipped." Drug addiction is a hard thing to beat.

One of the girls said she had been done for B & E (Breaking and Entering.) She had needed money for drugs. I asked if she had considered prostitution, since it isn't illegal. Don't worry, *I wasn't recommending it.*

She looked shocked. "I couldn't do that! I love my boyfriend."

I had to think about that one for a while.

3. I have really benefitted from the rest. I must be careful not to get lazy. I do three sets of fifty sit ups each day, as we can't access the gym every day.

4. I have more time to myself.

5. Less to do, fewer rules, clearer rules, I get into less trouble. It's jail. It looks like jail; it feels like jail and we eat jail food, so there is little danger of over eating. I can relax.

6. I have caught up with a couple of my favorite chaplains and some other friends I had been wondering about.

On the downside, I'm not yet sure if I'd like visits from anyone but my family here. It's a long way, it's a lot of hassle for the visitors and it's not a nice visiting area. I preferred to "entertain" in the Helena Jones garden with coffee, tea, nice food and the illusion of normality. Jail is jail. There is nothing "pretty" here for you to enjoy. Bars, sniffer dogs, and razor wire fences are not very inviting.

Please keep emailing. It's so encouraging to receive mail. If I can encourage you in your battles, I will. You are stronger than you think. Don't let pride or disappointment hold you back. Ask honestly for His perspective and you will have peace.

Love you all so much,

Trish Jenkins xxxx

P.S. I rang the swine flu hotline; but all I got was crackling!!!

23rd Letter

10th July

Hello my friends,

"The Perils of Patricia" continue. I keep drafting letters to you and discarding them. My stories would take too long so I file my notes; ready to type out, when I leave here. Hopefully, my editor will consider my prison tales worth her efforts.

Thank you to those who have offered to send me books. Please don't, as they won't be given to me. When I left Helena Jones, I was in the middle of *'Secret Believers,'* a book about the persecution of Christians in the Arab world. I really have nothing to complain about, compared to them.

There are already lots of Christian books we can access, so I pick them up in between murder mysteries. I try to avoid romance novels at Wacol!

It's really important to have a method of handling setbacks so they don't escalate. I have become quite an expert at this, if I do say so myself.

Yesterday provided a traumatic experience. I was waiting for a visit from Mum and Dad, when I was informed it had to be a "non-contact" visit. No one would tell me why. It was my first visit since coming back here, so I didn't know if it was part of the punishment - along with being put into S1.

It had to be a mistake, as I am not a high-risk prisoner. I was not going to find out why until after and even then I may not be told. Was it possible that yet again I had done something wrong without realising it?

Had they found contraband, in my cell, left by a previous occupant? Had someone decided they didn't like me and said something to the Officers? Any of these things were possible.

"Non–contact" visits are like you see in the movies, but without the telephone. I waited on my side, trying not to cry. In the visitor's processing area, my parents were holding everyone up because their hardworking, flat fingertips were causing problems for the fingerprint reader....

It's a hard visit, when all parties know that there is the possibility of me getting in more trouble. If I get moved, my phone takes a week to get connected, so my family is left in limbo as the Prison won't tell them anything.

Recently, the chaplains were prohibited from making calls on our behalf. Mum did find out that if she asks for a counsellor, she has to be put through to one. Until then, she had been getting the run-around from Officer "not my problem."

Upon returning to my unit, I put in a request form asking why the visit was a "non-contact" visit. It's usually just the drug addicts, at risk of smuggling, who have those.

Mum is a feisty lady who fights for those she loves. Officers came to me, in the afternoon, to inform me that there had been a mistake made and would I please inform my mother as soon as possible so she would stop calling!

Good on you, Mum.

23rd Letter, continued

14th July

Sometimes, you are quietly walking along when someone runs up behind you, shoves you in the back, and the momentum plants your face in the dirt. Oof!

I must be "Queen of the Bounce Back," by now. Last night, I decided I would spend today in prayer and fasting. The Lord has given me some general directions and I wanted to wait on Him so I could begin to flush them out.

This morning, I found out that people, who could visit me at Helena Jones, would have to apply all over again, to visit me here. That means my parents are the only ones that can visit, and they are going away for five weeks. I don't know if it's true or just another "mistake."

At the same time, I received some lovely mail from some of you, which was great. Justin posting you emails is a fantastic way to enable people to shoot off little messages to me; I really appreciate it.

He prints them out and posts them on to me.

I'm not sure why being tipped back from Helena Jones, puts my visitors in a category that demands another application and hassle. So today, I got past the hurt of disappointment and anger at having so little control over my life, and focused on "bounce back." If it takes four to eight weeks to get visitors, so be it. I can focus on here and now.

This is where God has me. I will try not to focus on arbitrary bureaucracy and "surprise" rules. I'll try not to think about how much time is left. This is my world for now.

These are my people – the lonely, the sad, the immoral, the drug addicted, the brain fried, the broken, the ugly, the poor, the rebellious, the angry, and the violent. These are His daughters. They are my ministry.

Please pray that I am effective and not hindered by distractions from the enemy.

Deep breath, back straight, shoulders back – "once more into the breach" as they say...?

Love, Trish.

PS I just found out it was another "mistake." There is not a problem with HJ visitors coming here.

Don't give up, when you have similar "shoves in the back." Respond how you know you should and it will be resolved faster.

24th Letter

16th July

Hello Friends,

A rather disturbing and dramatic event occurred this afternoon. A group of officers turned up with a sniffer dog. We had already been locked in our cells since 10a.m. We'd been let out only long enough to make a sandwich which had to be taken immediately back into our cells with us.

We were called out and made to line up in our caged yard. The officer with the dog walked along in front of us, ordered us to step forward and then walked behind us. He ordered us to step back and then forward again, but he didn't pass by us again. Instead, he laughed at his joke on us.

Pathetic.

I don't know if the officers were trying to lighten a tense situation; but their idea of humour was to mock, swear at, and belittle us. Anyone, who tried to answer, was told, "You're prisoners; it's what you get."

So many retorts sprang to my mind; but I said nothing. They continued their mockery as they went from cell to cell, searching everything, and turning bedding upside down, carelessly tipping personal belongings onto the floor.

S1 is the maximum of maximum security; apart from the DU which is solitary confinement. This is what is necessary for them to find drugs or other contraband. It's hard to describe the indignity. I wouldn't mind so much, if they did not taunt us. I fixed memories in my mind of Corrie Ten Boom and concentration camps; to remind me that it's not that bad.

My heart was thumping hard. While lined up, I alternated between looking down (in order to let my hair fall around my face and in my eyes) so they would not look at me, or looking past them with my chin up. This is S1. Bad language and intimidation are a given, but I don't like hearing it from the officers; the supposed "non-criminals."

One of the officers was a wiry, little bald man with a goatee. He seemed to take particular delight in humiliating us. I remember him visiting Helena Jones and making a smart comment about "setting the dogs on us." He was particularly rude to visitors to the prison as well; though he's not the only one. Visitors don't complain for fear of retribution against their loved one.

In my mind I was saying, "It's a small man who humiliates those without power." To my chagrin, I had actually muttered this out loud!

An officer stepped towards me, "What did you say about 'small'?" Presumably, he was looking for a challenge.

Fortunately, there was a distraction and things moved on.

We were required to line up for the dog again. Three women had been strip searched, thankfully not me; our rooms were a mess, and we were each escorted back to our cells and locked in again.

I am told it's not as bad as it used to be. Not so long ago, the officers would empty every bottle of shampoo, conditioner, or moisturiser onto the floor, along with precious letters and photos. The girls would be left in tears and needing to purchase all the bottled liquids again. Not easy when wages are about $26 a week and items are full retail price. Thankfully, they don't beat up the girls anymore, at least not without provocation.

We ended up being locked in our cells from 10a.m. to 5p.m. It was a dark tormented day for some of these poor women.

They didn't find anything.

The "everyday" officers in S1 can be rude; but are OK for the most part. I guess they see there is no point provoking already volatile women, and then being stuck with them for a whole shift!

I think of a young woman who did something so dumb I am convinced she was mentally defective. She then wanted me to pray for her protection. I said I could; but she needed me to pray for her to be less rebellious, as that was causing all her problems, including her current predicament.

She said, "No, I don't want that."

So, I said, "I can't help you then; my prayers would be pointless."

I got a new perspective on the term "to cast pearls before swine." Details after I get out.

While the other women were at work, this girl had socialised with two women in the unit next door. The result was that she gave them tattoos. Not just any tattoos; but little swastikas on their upper arms!

I had spent the afternoon in my cell and was unaware of what happened, until I heard a "subdued commotion." It was a serious and dangerous drama; but nobody wanted the officers to know about it.

What made it dangerous was that the two women lived with Shona, a highly feared, Aboriginal woman. That afternoon, the two women were hiding in their cells and the tattoo "artist" was claiming she had no idea it would offend our black flatmates.

Shona paced up and down the cage slowly and silently with her nostrils flaring. Once again I was captivated. Occasionally, someone tried to speak to her; but she ignored them.

Eventually, it was time for us to go inside. The others went in and I felt compelled to reach out to Shona.

"Shona," I began. She looked at me. I continued, my heart thumping, "You know I'm a Christian." She nodded curtly. She'd never spoken to me before or even bothered to acknowledge me.

"I can't even imagine the pain you must be feeling right now." Now, I had her attention. "I want you to know that I don't hold with what happened today. God sees you as just as valuable as

anyone else. You are precious to Him and He loves you... Well, I just wanted to tell you that."

She just nodded at me and I went inside. The next day, I was transferred out of there.

I saw this precious woman again, some weeks later, at a head-count in the education block. Others greeted her enthusiastically, because she is one of the two toughest, most feared Aborigines here.

She ignored them; but then spotted me. "Hey Trish, how are ya, Sista-girl?" I smiled and stood a little straighter, "Great, thanks Shona, good to see you again!"

The others looked at me as if to ask, "Who the hell are you???"

It was a most satisfying feeling.

25th Letter

21st July

This morning, I was moved back to the normal secure building. It holds four units. I'm back in S7, the Induction Unit, which is the very first one I was in.

I remember how nervous I was the first time around. This time, I opened the door and smiled at the first face I saw.

Different women, same issues.

I went out into the yard, knowing the group would be sizing me up. I had an ace up my sleeve, as I sat down on the metal bench and stared back.

"So, where'd *you* come from?" They demanded belligerently.

With a steely face and a quiet, firm voice I said, "Just did three weeks in S1."

A collective "Ooh!" arose. Eyebrows rose and the tone changed to one of awe and respect.

It was great, until someone who recognised me chirped, "Did you do something religious again?"

"No; I was bad and that's where the bad girls go." It's not something I'm proud of, but they were all suitably impressed and respectful. Go figure.

My new room is brighter, and my TV reception is clear. A lot of TV's have aerials with broken wire that has been stuffed with foil. They get sabotaged by women exposing the wire and making a spark with a battery for their cigarettes!

I also started work this week. We were escorted over to a sweat-shop where we turn second-hand clothes into rags. We didn't really sweat; but we did work hard. I was allocated scissors and told to cut buttons and logos off.

Apparently, there were no "sales" positions available here!

There is strong animosity, between the white and black girls here; but I'm not part of it. I pretend not to see it, and the black girls see me differently, because of my reputation. Others have tough reputations. Mine is that I am spiritually gifted, a bit weird, but well-intentioned and harmless; also that I am afraid of no one. Go figure!

It's nice not having a camera in my room any more. It would not surprise me if some officers watch those of us, with no privacy, for entertainment. Their lack of respect, in front of us, makes me wonder just how badly they behave in their own lives.

I have no doubt that many of them have "habits" not much different to the inmates, morals included.

They can't blame "the job," as there are some quite decent officers too.

Ah well. I say nothing, observe everything, write in my journal, and mind my own business.

25th Letter, continued

22nd July

I tried to order a BRW (*Business Review Weekly*) magazine; but was knocked back. We are only allowed the intellectual strength of fashion and gossip magazines.

In terms of radio, I was impressed that one of the two radio stations we can access is 96.5 FM Family radio.

I try to wake up early enough for Charles Swindoll at 5.30. After that, it's great to hear Robbie and the others on the morning program.

Robbie belongs to the same church as me. When I hear his voice, I remember chatting with him as we queued to pick up our kids from children's church on Sunday.

It's a thin thread to the outside world.

Till next time.

Love to all,

Trish

26th Letter

24th July

Hello Friends,

Moved again! After just two nights in S7, I've moved straight over to "Residential." There is much more freedom of movement here. The buildings look like townhouses, from the outside.

I like it. After three weeks in the claustrophobic darkness of S1, this feels luxurious; even though inside it still feels like a unit in old-style Townsville; i.e., bare floors and painted besser block walls.

We can't walk on the grass, except for the patch which has the cigarette lighter post, but we can see it.

There is a tennis court with a net and we can walk around it anytime. There is a small gym.

We can visit the library almost every day. In S1, we had no library visits. Instead, the librarian would visit twice a week, with a small selection of books on a trolley.

Instead of bars on the windows, there are security grills that don't open. From my bedroom (cell) window, I can actually see a public road running past and paddocks beyond. I can look out, and see the outside world and cars going past; people with lives that are beyond the triple, razor wire fences.

On Monday I'll have eight weeks to go. It is the downhill run.

Last Monday I was still in S1 lamenting that I had lost the trim figure and fitness I had worked so hard for. I was seriously considering giving up trying and waiting until my final two weeks to starve myself back into shape. Not a wise plan.

Now, I have a new lease on life. I even received study papers so I can get my Certificate IV in Training and Assessment, thanks to my wonderful friend and previous employer, Vicky Jennings of www.ipspeople.com. I already had a high school teaching qualification. The Cert. IV is relevant to the vocational training of adults in and out of the workplace.

I like most of my unit mates. One is a dark girl with the most beautiful mahogany sheen to her skin. Another is a young mother of five children, who drove her car unlicensed, because she couldn't afford the registration and had no one to pick the kids up from school, one day.

Having a job and needing to drive to work can mean the difference between being allowed to drive and not allowed to drive. Being a mother needing to drive children to school, is not considered as important as being employed.

Having a job, at all, can keep you out of jail. However, the job of "mothering" is not considered important enough to do the same.

Catching up with old friends was nice. Since I'm considered a real "straighty," they couldn't believe I'd been tipped back.

"Did you get to go to Warwick?"

"Yeah, but I got kicked out."

"What about the cemetery work?"

"Yes; but I... um... got kicked out of that too."

They howled with laughter, as I recounted my litany of embarrassing experiences. I was too embarrassed and upset to write about them, at the time. Some stories are best kept for "ladies" meetings.

Helena Jones Centre fosters an atmosphere of tattle-taling. It helps them control the women. As naive as I might be; I could see through this manipulation and the hypocrisy that went on.

On the outside, I would not hesitate to call "Crime-Stoppers," but I made up my mind before I went in that I would not be a "dobber."

It probably didn't help that under questioning from the supervisor, I told her this to her face. She had wanted to know who was giving me a hard time. "I can't say," I answered.

"Can't, or won't?" she asked.

I looked at her steadily.

"Won't."

Images of "Cool Hand Luke" floated through my mind and I tried not to smile. We were having a *"failure to communicate."* It was all so ridiculously surreal.

I remember laughing (on the inside), at myself in this predicament.

Her face hardened.

"Well, you can wipe that smirk off your face!"

Oh dear.

Have you ever felt like, "If it weren't for bad luck, I'd have no luck at all?" Just kidding! It must be my Irish heritage coming out.

Until next time,

Love,

Trish

27th Letter

31st July

Hi all,

This letter is a bit eclectic as I wrote it over a few weeks.

I've been in Residential for almost two weeks now. It is the best of all the places I've been. More freedom, less pressure, no cages! Perhaps, it is also I who has changed. The other women complain about our restrictions and lock-downs; but to me this is luxury. In a Residential lock-down, we can still access our kitchen and common room; we just can't go outside. What lock-down?

Your status in prison defines your rights and privileges. Women can confuse it with social status. While returning from a circuit's workout at the gym, we passed Workshop 1. I knew my friends from Secure and S1 would be in there. One of my companions asked another one about it.

"That's the Secure Workshop. They're animals," was the scornful answer.

I experienced a defensive flash of anger. I quietly said, "Well, everyone in "Residential" has been a part of "Secure" first. Some people at Helena Jones think the same thing about us here. I know. I was there."

Why do people feel the need to consider they are either better than, or not as good as, someone else? Pride? Insecurity?

In God's economy, every single person is of infinite value. Social status is a man-made concept. I may have better manners, better skills, even a better functioning brain, but I am not of more worth, than the least of these!

I often laugh at myself. To become a police officer, only a Year 10 pass used to be required. The women here sometimes remark that prison officers are those who failed to become police officers. The argument may have some merit. I can't think of anyone who would say, "As a child I wanted to grow up and become a corrections officer!" Who knows?

Before I look down my nose, I am reminded of the side of the razor wire on which I currently live! Hence, I laugh at myself…

I'd asked an officer at HJC why we are called "offenders," as though we are "offensive." I found it insulting.

"Well, it's politically correct."

"What makes it politically correct? Or the other words like 'prisoner,' incorrect?"

"Well, it's… I don't know! Why would you ask?"

Is it any wonder they sent me back here?

I had an interesting chat with a twenty-one-year-old drug addicted, single mother of three. Well, she's not currently using drugs. I asked her how old she was when she started going off the rails.

"About fourteen," she answered.

"Was it because of the influence of your peer group?"

"No, it was the people I was hanging around; they offered it to me."

Right.

The cost of rebellion is greater than we think.

In contrast, a little Aboriginal girl had math books out at the dining table. I made a wrong assumption.

"Are you completing high school?"

"No. It's a bridging course for university. I did two years of Uni for my nursing degree; but it was so long ago I have to start over. I got side-tracked when my mum died, and I turned to drugs as I couldn't cope."

That night, and the following night, I had the privilege of praying for this lovely young woman. Her Christian family already prays for her to return to Christ. Now, she has renewed faith and healing in her heart.

Some people dismiss "jail house" religion as insincere. Sometimes it is. However, sometimes it takes prison to get someone still long enough to listen to the Lord calling them. He meets us in our darkest hour. Of course, He is in the prisons. His presence is very powerful here.

May the fear of the Lord come upon you, so there is no need for Him to take drastic action to get your attention! Is life tough for you right now? Maybe "life" is trying to talk to you. Beware of being too "busy" to listen.

One of the girls in our unit excitedly announced she had only seven weeks to go. I was happy, as I was reminded that my exit is seven weeks from Monday.

"That's right," she said. "I'm four days after you."

"Hold on, you're the 25th and I'm the 21st."

"Yes."

I checked my calendar. Oh dear. I didn't have the heart to tell her, she actually has eight weeks to go. I'll know when she has worked it out, because I will hear the expletives from anywhere on the property.

One young woman was in jail for nine months for driving unlicensed. It sounds like a tough sentence; but it was the seventh time she'd been caught.

Another one said, "Yeah, I'm in here, 'coz I got caught driving when my rego had run out. Of course, I was also unlicensed and the drugs they found in the car didn't help..."

Sometimes you see footage on the news of an armed hold-up of a bottle shop, or service station. I sat and listened while a pretty girl entertained us with stories of what it's like to be the robber. It's almost always for drug money.

This one said she used to sing in church, but when I quizzed her I realised it was a strange, controlling cult. Unfortunately, she wasn't interested in the difference. I can't rescue all the starfish on the beach... I just watch and listen and wait for the ones who are meant to cross my path.

I've met one or two women who rebelled against strict parents, but mostly these women had parents who were permissive or just too busy to stop and handle the pre-teen stage. Yes, "pre-teen."

Most of the women I've talked to about when they started to go off the rails, said ages ten to twelve. By thirteen to fourteen, the peer group provided their code of behaviour.

"Jill hit puberty at twelve and decided that meant it was time to do something about her crush on her brother's twenty-five-year-old friend. He obliged. I suggested to Jill, "Do you realise that makes him a sexual predator? You could sue him, or even have him put in jail."

"Why would I do that?" she asked in surprise. "He's a mate!" Apparently, many girls believe their first menstruation is the green light for intercourse.

At fourteen, Kate was riding around in stolen vehicles, trying out whatever drugs were available. Girls fighting provided entertainment for the boys, who of course, they want to impress.

Taking drugs as an adolescent can permanently damage the brain. I see the evidence of that as I talk with some of the girls. One has speed-induced schizophrenia, another ADHD and another has bi-polar disorder triggered by drug use.

Their ability to use logic to connect consequences to their actions is impaired. They are not so crazy that they need to be put in a mental ward, but there is no doubt they will keep coming back to jail.

How do you help someone who lacks the ability to reason? Someone who thinks rebellion is cool? No one is in here applauding, so where is the reward for their self-destruction?

27th Letter, continued

9th August

I've moved again. Residential is made up of two clusters of buildings. One day, a "Forby" (rhyming slang: 4 b 2= screw= officer) asked me how I was going. I was immediately suspicious; as such a question is out of character for officers. "Fine, thanks."

"You are very quiet."

"Just minding my business; I'm quite happy here."

The next day, I was moved to the rear cluster. It's quieter, and houses the more long term residents and some older ladies.

I like my new unit. The women are less volatile and more considerate of one another. It makes me smile to think about the kinds of women I live with. They are "long-termers" for a reason. I remember reading about the Lesbian Vampire Killer twenty years ago, and here I am, lining up with her. Another one the press labelled "the Black Widow" hands me my library books!

I'll chat to people as I find them; but I don't go out of my way to make friends or "rescue" anyone. Some of the older ladies look so sweet, they are clearly educated, well-mannered, but happen to also be skilled con-artists and even murderers. All have a story.

I have been able to slot into some study which rescues me from the rag-shop, *two days there was enough*. Doing roughly a unit each week, I should get half of a Certificate III in Business Admin completed, plus the Cert. IV in Training and Assessment.

Thank you to those who have written and emailed me. Justin forwards me your messages faithfully.

Well, I'm off to do more laps of the tennis court. I don't run as much these days, as I quickly get pain in my calves. I'm told it's a combination of running on concrete and the $7 Kmart sneakers they issued us.

Such is life.

Oh, I caught up with my French acquaintance from S9. I tried to explain my return, in broken French; but the most accurate phrase I could come up with was, "Tres merd!"

Roughly translated, it means "a spot of bother"... or something like that!

Love, Trish

28th Letter

17th August

Dear Friends,

It would be easy for me to become hard in here. There are some genuinely nasty people; but they are not always the ones who have committed the worst crimes.

I am quite lucky in my unit. No one is openly hostile, unless they feel provoked. I live with two murderers, three frauds and a druggie. I don't know the details of all their stories and I don't need to. Some have been in jail previously.

I don't know if this is the last leg of my journey, as a lot can change in a week, even a day. Different ones come and go. My heart is breaking for the two women who have taken lives. They suffer such torment over what they have done.

Unless you are given the same history and set of circumstances, you cannot say if you would do the same as they. These are nice, respectable, middle class women. I can't say much more than that. I am praying for healing in their hearts and minds and for wisdom.

Talk of faith, even God's love, is not generally welcome for all kinds of reasons. I am also aware of the mental instability that lives just beneath a calm façade of so many women here.

I do hope my remaining time is not wasted. While I concentrate on my own personal and professional development, I hope I don't overlook the person who needs a word of comfort. In the last few days, I sensed a hardening in my heart. It happens from time to time, when I can't help but notice cruel or bitchy behaviour between the women.

I rarely say anything; but on the inside I disapprove and feel judgemental towards them. Sometimes the victim is a friend, or one of those defenceless people that society rejects. Sometimes they are a bit slow or otherwise "odd." Sometimes they are "normal" and the discord is simply the result of living in close proximity with others.

Anyway, I got alone with God and sorted myself out. Repentance again and asking Him to show me these women through His eyes. Prayers like those work immediately. A couple of women who knew me from S9 have commented that I had changed.

Prison will do that. One of them was concerned that my spirit might have been broken, because I seemed quieter. The other liked me better. She found it hard to explain why; but she said I used to be too interested in everybody.

I am a lot more circumspect in my dealings with people. I am mindful that keeping to myself can make me grow selfish. It's not my job to try to lift everyone out of the pit. Yet I don't want to overlook the ones who have been placed in my path.

Many of these women have had just enough religious experience to put them off church. Some of them feel like no amount of prison can make up for what they have done. That's true, but how do I explain the power in the Blood that washes their sin away, even for murder, without it sounding like a cliché?

That is where prayer and the Holy Spirit come in. Without those, I could do more damage than good. During my journey, I have several times been to the point of "Though He slay me, yet will I trust Him" Job 13:15.

As strange as it may sound, to those of you who don't know Him, that end point of surrender is the turning point.

I don't despair; I am not depressed or anxious anymore. The Psalmist wrote, "I would have despaired had I not believed that I would see the goodness of the Lord, in the land of the living!" (Psalm 27:13).

When everyday Christians don't live as "Overcomers," you can imagine how much harder it is in here. Yet, still the light shines in the darkness.

Only a supernatural force can do that.

Without it, prison is as Oscar Wilde described,

> "The vilest deeds
>
> Like poisonous weeds
>
> Bloom well in prison air.
>
> 'Tis only what is good in man
>
> That dies and withers there."

That old reprobate is one of my favourite writers.

Our prisons are not as dismal as they were in Oscar's day. He never recovered from his experience. I can dispel a couple of myths regarding jail. One is the assumption that prisoners get out after their "minimum" term, if they have been good. When we read of a fifteen-year sentence, to be eligible for parole after eight; we feel incredulous at the discrepancy.

Being eligible for parole simply means they can begin to apply. The process takes months and some women have been applying for years. Fortunately, it doesn't apply to me. I cannot be held to ransom with the threat of a longer stay.

One of the inconsistencies of the legal system is the discrepancy of sentencing between white collar, non-violent crime; and violent, sexual assault. I'd like to see an investigation comparing the two areas. One could be forgiven for thinking our judicial system values money more than our children. Or is there something more sinister behind it?

The other myth is that we are spoilt, with access to TV and a gym and able to purchase things like chocolate. It's true we have these things; but we have them only so that they can be taken away!

People who refuse to work have their TV taken away. People who misbehave have restricted access to the "buy up" form - only bathroom products and stationery.

Living in Residential, without a cage around your unit, is a privilege and women get "tipped back" for breaching any rules. It's a fairly effective behaviour management strategy. I've had the privilege of experiencing almost everything our penal system has to offer!

The best thing about my unit is Marge, the lady who elected to do the cooking. She makes a cooked lunched for us, as she doesn't work in the mornings. The evenings are "catch and kill," but she will often make a desert. She is a kind and thoughtful middle-aged lady with grown up sons. *It's hard to imagine she killed her husband, though I did see her lose her temper once or twice; it was illogical and quite nasty.*

A similar aged lady was home today and helped with lunch. I asked Marge if she enjoyed having company in the kitchen for a change. She answered, "Yes," and I commented, "Well, you both seem to have a lot in common!" I paused and realised what I'd said.

They looked at each other and then at me "Do you mean because we both have grown sons, or because we're both in for the same thing?" ... I'd forgotten that they had both killed their husbands...Oops! It was actually, awkwardly funny.

I went to music group today. Choir once a week will be fun. All was going well. We did a few exercises, sang a couple of songs and then the "education officer" played a CD of "I Dreamed a Dream" from *"Les Miserables."*

To my dismay, it reached in and tore my heart out. By the time it ended, I was a weeping, embarrassed mess. The song could apply to any one of us, as it is about broken dreams.

The funny thing was they said, "Don't worry; we've all had a song do that to us in here!"

One last story: I speak to my family almost every day. I don't usually write about them, as it's a private part of my life. However, I'd like to share this. One of our twins, Felicity said, "Mummy, I love you, I want to hug you!"

"Well sweetie," I answered, "You know how a cake is made of egg and flour and stuff?"

"Yes."

"Well, you and your sisters are made of Mummy and Daddy, so if you hug your sister, you are hugging a part of me."

I was on speaker phone and all I could here was the sound the twins make when they embrace each other, "Aaaah."

"Better now?"

"Yes, mummy."

Soon, I will be hugging my family in the flesh. Nothing else matters.

Take care of you and yours.

Love,

Trish xxxx

My arrival home – back with my family

If you look closely, you will notice how far the blond hair grew out. 8 months of hair regrowth is not pretty, but we didn't care. All that mattered was being together.

This photo was taken on the same day, however, I didn't realise it had been taken.

I came across this picture some months later in my mother's camera.

I was shocked to see the toll of prison written on my face.

Over a period of months, with love and healing, I became well again.

29th Letter

28th August

Dear friend,

I write with a heavy heart.

"I thought I had it tough when I had no shoes;

Until I met a man who had no feet."

This morbid little saying is powerful.

Thinking of it usually gives me a grateful, happier perspective; at least it did until I began praying for a "footless" woman here. Then I found myself interceding with tears.

It was a tough week that seemed to drag and was spotted with annoyances that now seem trivial. Then one evening I sat with Gayle, who is eight months pregnant. She is doing everything she can to improve herself with courses and counselling. We sat at the bottom of my unit's stairs.

As she talked, I lifted her feet into my lap to massage them, trying to bring her comfort. There was nothing I could say. Gayle was already booked in to have her baby by caesarean section. She had no choice about that, because Corrective Services has to plan the security roster required.

That was fine, but you see, Gayle has been informed that when her child is born, she will return to prison without her baby.

The authorities have decided to take it away. She won't be joining the mothers' unit.

It's even more distressing, because the sentencing judge had given her an extra eight weeks, so she could look after her new baby in the safety and security of prison. Now, she won't have her child but will still serve the extra two months.

It's so wrong. I can't imagine a greater horror, then going to hospital in labour, and in hand cuffs, only to have the child from my womb taken away, in a decision made by bureaucrats.

As we sat, I asked her what I could do for her.

"Please pray they let me keep my baby here with me, at least till I get out." *Gayle is familiar with C.O.C. but never really committed her life to Christ.*

I was not praying for a simple headache or a job. This was about the destiny of two people.

I said to her, "I will pray. I can't say that God will answer our prayers exactly how we want Him to. He knows all things. What I can say is that you can trust Him."

I prayed for her and her baby to stay together. I even had a prophetic word for the little one. It's funny how the gifts of the Spirit emerge even when you don't expect them.

I am torn between sorrow for her situation and joy that God is moving in her life. Please pray for her in agreement with me. This one thing I know: We don't always get what we want, but we can always trust Him.

I love the Serenity Prayer:

> "God grant me the serenity to
>
> Accept the things I cannot change,
>
> Courage to change the things I can,
>
> And the wisdom to know the difference."

The real problem for people is in not knowing the difference.

I can't change being here, but I can change how I look at it.

Have the courage to change your perspective on your situation.

Then you'll know whether it's the situation that needs to change, or if it's you who needs to change.

Much love,

Trish

30th Letter

1st September

Hi,

I finished reading a book called *"The Prisoner in the 3rd Cell"* by Gene Edwards. It's a fictional account of John the Baptist's rough life and last days. Its point is to trust God even when He doesn't meet your expectations.

Long ago I realised, if we are ever disappointed with God, it's never His fault. He doesn't change; we just had wrong expectations. God is not my puppet. He is not obliged to do my will, regardless of how good I am or how much I give.

A prominent businessman once said to me, "If someone is not paying your account, it means there is sin in your life!" I'm sure the Pharisees would have agreed, but I don't.

Evangelicals are particularly susceptible to "cause and effect" thinking. We want a formula for success and we want something to blame, when things are not going our way. Why? So we can control our circumstances. It's not unlike old fashioned superstition.

Sometimes sin is the cause of a lack of prosperity or unanswered prayer. The Bible says a man who mistreats his wife will not have his prayers answered.

If your business is suffering from a high turnover of staff, perhaps you have a "management issue"; i.e., a bad temper driving them away.

Yet, the wicked still prosper. We are instructed not to envy them. There are some things about God we will never understand, to be able to do so would make us equal with Him and that is absurd. To think it is even possible is the height of arrogance.

It's only after we make up our minds to trust Him by faith that a measure of understanding comes. Ironically, when it does, it's not so important!

I'm no hero. I still get caught up by little frustrations; but I'm learning to ask for His perspective on each matter at earlier points than I used to.

For example, I've been waiting weeks to get new sneakers, as the ones I was issued with, in January, are falling apart. Uniform replacements are supposed to happen on Tuesdays but they don't always call it, and if you are in class, you are not allowed to leave class, which usually includes attendance on Tuesdays...

I felt sorry for one woman here who has around ten years to serve. She complained about several things, when she first arrived. Perhaps she thought if she was going to be here a long time, she would make sure she had her rights. Fair enough.

Funnily enough, her order for shoes has been unfilled for the last six months. Yet others of the same size have come and gone since...must be a clerical error...

You have the right to complain, but you'd better count the cost.

Finally, last Tuesday I trotted off, relieved but without high expectations. Of the two styles available, neither fit me. They also look like they had been specifically chosen so that nobody would want to steal them! My broken down shoes suddenly held more appeal.

Rather than be annoyed, I simply lined them with sanitary pads and went off for my run as usual. Having a sense of humour and being flexible saves a lot of angst.

It's important to know what the problem really is. I thought my problem was not being able to get new shoes. I couldn't solve that. When I realised the real problem was discomfort, I could solve that.

Is your problem your circumstance? Or is it your perspective of your circumstance? Learn to adapt quickly and have a sense of humour.

If you struggle with being a self-righteous, know-it-all "it's not fair" sour-puss, ask the Lord for His perspective. He's probably already laughing!

31ˢᵗ Letter

14ᵗʰ September

Dear Friends.

I have finally hit the last week of my stay. I had recently become somewhat apprehensive of the next stage of my life, as there are those who view people who've been in jail, as a worse kind of sinner, then the Lord led me again to Romans 6 through 8. It's God's opinion that counts, not Man's.

I'm sure I've met every kind of person in here. I often forget how dangerous it has been. Recently, a friend of mine got into a fight and was punched in the throat. I've never felt physically in danger; but I have met some really nasty people.

Even when I had resisted a particular woman who had minions of support, by the time we parted company, I could see she had a grudging respect for me. We had eventually been required to work on an art project together, just before I was "tipped." I had kept my own self-respect; albeit at a price.

I've had people turn on me but I know it is more about their issues and mental illness than about me. This happened in my very last week and was particularly vicious. I stayed calm and apologised for "making them feel that way, it wasn't my intention."

The result was a fizzling out of the energy. It reminded me of the proverb, "A soft word turns away wrath." It was disturbing, but a couple of other women said I'd handled it the best way possible.

In happier news, the lady we prayed for to be allowed to keep her baby was given permission to do so.

I prefer the company of the really bad girls over the sneaky stuck-up ones. "Bad" is a relative term. Many of them are "lovable rogues," quite harmless, but you wouldn't give them your home address.

One is in for drugs and is a prostitute, because the money is so good. She says, "When the perverts are with me they are not touching a little kid!" It's quite a noble sentiment, when you think about it.

Over the time, I've introduced quite a number of people to Jesus and ministered healing to the broken hearted. Some will stay free and some will keep coming back, no different to church people returning to their own issues. Constantly, but gradually, being delivered from their fears and hang-ups.

We should not prejudge individuals, but it's foolish to ignore danger signs.

Here are a handful of practical things I've learned;

Have a lock on your letterbox; lots of people go for walks and collect your mail looking for credit card details.

If a young woman knocks on your door saying, "Please help me, I was adopted and this is the last known address of my mother," run inside and check your back door, because her partner will be inside looking for your wallet!"

The really successful drug traffickers do not often go to jail; they live in posh suburbs like Hamilton and Ascot.

Middle and upper class houses are popular with "sneaks" – A "sneak" is a person who robs a house while the occupant is home. It's easy, because they don't have to break in and it gives them a thrill. It's particularly popular with school kids at holiday time.

Unlicensed driving is rampant. It's not just rev-heads; many are the mothers of young schoolchildren. Keep your insurance up to date, as they won't have any.

No matter how bad someone is, it's never too late for them. Prison is not the end. Jesus spends a lot of time here reaching people whom you would never expect to receive Him.

Stay humble; remember you are only one bad car accident from prison yourself. Only the Grace of God keeps us from walking in someone else's shoes.

I encourage you to be generous and kind, but be smart about your charity. Don't blindly follow any leader, employer or pastor, no matter how successful, especially if they spend a lot of time talking about their success.

Truly successful people don't need to boast, and they don't need your money.

I have been through quite a tribulation but I can honestly say that the Lord has made it worthwhile.

I am so grateful to those of you who have helped my family stay strong and happy.

I don't know what the future holds, but I am confident my experience will not be wasted. God is a good God; it's people who can be a bit strange!

If you see me at conference, I may look a little lost, so please come and say, "Hello."

Bless you heaps,

Trish Jenkins xxx

FREEDOM PRAYER:

If you have been touched or challenged by the spiritual aspects of this book, it's quite likely your spirit is nudging you. If not, just skip to the Epilogue.

God's purpose for your life is good. He wants you healthy, prosperous, in sound mind and serving mankind with your gifts, whatever they are. Most of all, He wants a personal relationship with you.

I invite you to ask Jesus Christ into your heart, with a simple prayer of reconnection:

"Heavenly Father, I thank you that you love me. I ask you to forgive me for the wrong choices I've made. Your Son, Jesus, paid the price for my sin, by His death on the cross.

Dear Jesus, death could not hold you and you rose again.

I hand my entire life over to you; my family, my work and my relationships.

I am forgiven. Now, as I am forgiven, please take any poison of hate out of my life. I now choose to forgive.... (Name the people that you need to forgive, then release them to God and He will deal with them.)

Even more, Lord, in spite of what they did, I ask you to bless them in their mind, their health, their family and their finances. They no longer hold power over my emotions, I hand them over to You.

I ask for your Holy Spirit to give me wisdom and guidance. Help me to make right choices. Make my desires, your desires.

Lord, give me your perspective on... (Talk to Him about your situation, things you are concerned about).

Thank you for coming into my life.

In Jesus' Name, Amen.

You now have a Friend who is "closer than a brother." Talk to Him about everything; commit your ways to Him and He will direct your path.

Find a modern Bible and start reading from Matthew.

Then find a church that enjoys God, loves people, reads the Word, and feels right for you. Listen to your gut (spirit) to help you decide.

Now find a need and fill it! ☺

I pray your personal journey brings you fulfilment and that your legacy makes the world a better place.

Epilogue

I did return to the arms of my family and my church. I was emotionally bruised, but happy. I knew I would require some ministry, as my mind and emotions were all out of whack. My perspective was shot.

I hadn't realised how damaged I was, until I saw a photograph of myself taken when I arrived home. Hugging my children, glad to be there; but in my eyes, the brokenness showed.

The beautiful thing about brokenness is that the Lord is near us. He is sometimes all we have. My family loved me but they would never understand the toll taken on me.

Prison was a bubble with limited issues to deal with. The outside world frightened me. There is no guidance, no debrief for prisoners, prior to release. There is rehab for drug addicts and some must report to parole officers; but there is no orientation about what to expect, or what emotions I would feel. There were only leaflets for women who were returning to an abusive home and phone numbers for Social Services, none of which I qualified for.

There was not even a leaflet my family could pick up to warn them that I might not act like the same person they knew before... and I wasn't the same. I was damaged and I felt tainted.

I had expected that after such a tough time, nothing could upset me ever again. Instead, it felt like I was badly bruised and the slightest touch caused pain. At the same time, normal customer service in a shop moved me close to tears, as I was not used to being spoken to as though I mattered.

I wanted to put the horrible story behind me and move on, as if nothing had happened. So I put my notes and letters in a box under my sofa. I am ashamed to say, I couldn't even bring myself to write to the women back in prison. Not even to send a Christmas card. It was selfish, but I was broken.

I had unexplainable outbursts of either tears or anger. I was tormented by nightmares of being stuck in prison with no one listening to my insistence that I didn't belong there anymore. In another nightmare, I was silently trying to escape, lest they find me and keep me there. I would awaken shaken, frightened and fragile.

My life was like a jar of river water that had been shaken up. The sediment needed time to settle, for the clarity of the water to return.

I wanted to find a job, love my family, and be invisible. I felt I had "done my bit" for the Gospel. Hadn't I fulfilled my calling as much as I could?

I had been through a "Joseph" experience; but there was no Pharaoh offering me a position.

Oh, I still had dreams of doing great things but I doubted they would be allowed to come to anything. If they did, it could only be by the intervention of the Almighty.

I applied for a number of jobs with little success. Even stacking shelves at a supermarket requires a criminal history check! An ex-offender is not obliged to disclose their record, but must answer honestly if the question is asked.

Some days were better than others. Then, like a wave coming up from behind, the "feeling" of prison would sweep over me unexpectedly and drench me.

I had to create new, positive memories to replace the ones taking up space in my mind.

I took surfing lessons, sat outside in the sun and played with my girls.

A New Phase

Gradually, I began to heal. As I spent time in prayer and meditation, a growing thought persisted. I was reminded of the sense of destiny that had sustained me in prison. If there is a plan for my life, why would it end at the prison gate?

For the most part I had been fearless in prison. Why should I be frightened now? If I believed that God works all things together for good, would He not weave something good out of my story?

I began to feel a conviction that there were lessons in my story worth sharing. In fact, if I did not use it to benefit others, my experience would be rendered pointless.

I couldn't live with that.

I had an unfinished manuscript about fraud signals. How could I publish a book without people finding out I went to prison?

I also had the makings of another manuscript based on my letters from prison and journal entries.

Would the world be interested in one woman's prison journey? Would anyone be interested in what God can do, in the darkest of places where the "undesirables" live?

Could I dare to publish a book and have the whole world find out my failure? I wrestled with God and my pride.

I finally accepted not only that I could, but that *I must!*

That was April 2010. Immediately, I felt a burden lift, replaced by a passion. The decision gave me courage.

Ironically, I received a job offer shortly afterwards. It was in sales, my field. Great commissions, local territory and everything I would have jumped at just 1 month earlier.

Taking a deep breath, I politely turned it down, explaining I had made a choice to strike out on my own and had to give it a go.

2010 was an extraordinary year. I received much mental and emotional healing. I finished writing my previous book, gained a qualification in training and started networking to promote my upcoming book.

One day at a marketing seminar, I was picked out to stand in front of 500 people. I'd said I was a fraud prevention expert and the presenter challenged me with:

"So what makes you any different from anyone else in your field?"

I took the microphone, looked at the crowd, and said, "Well, I don't know anyone else, who does what I do, and has been to prison."

You could have heard a pin drop. To this day, I meet people who were in that meeting who tell me how they were touched.

It was the beginning of a speaking career that allows me to impact people from all walks of life.

God preserved me through a tribulation. He had broken me down, moulded, chiselled, sanded and strengthened me. The process of development did not stop, when I got home, but went on for at least another year.

I'm sure it will continue for the rest of my life.

My family were wonderfully supportive. My husband was amazing, considering he had his own grief and anger issues to deal with over our experience. My children were extremely tolerant of my erratic emotions, while I balanced out.

Eventually, the Lord turns our mourning into dancing. But it won't happen without our cooperation. We must choose to make our past serve us and use it to serve others. In doing so, we beat that rotten "devil" at his own game!

The enemy tried to silence me. He has failed and he will pay.

It took all my courage, but it's worth it.

I continue to make a difference.

I like the person I have become more than the person I was when we were "successful."

Back then, I had "answers."

Now I know what matters.

I live "on purpose." My experience enables me to reach and impact people I never could before.

Little hinges swing big doors. Little decisions can have massive consequences, or results.

May your little decisions build your life and not tear it down.

Live on purpose. Make a difference.

You can, because you matter.

You *must,* because we matter!

We need you.

"You Can Change the Past and Free Your Future"

This is me talking to a group of businesspeople. It was filmed by Channel 10 for prime time evening news!

See the cameraman in the background?

I am not just a motivational speaker, my story changes lives.

I had the courage to believe in my purpose and you can too.

There is a purpose for your life and it's a good one. Don't let shame rob the rest of us of your contribution!

In a few short months I've shared on radio, TV and in newspapers.

If I make a difference, all the crap will be worth it!

You matter - You have value – We need You!

Life after jail makes good tale

ABOUT THE AUTHOR

Trish Jenkins is a dynamic inspirational, motivational speaker to business and interest groups. She is an authority on fraud signals and overcoming adversity. Her first book, *"Dangerous Wealth: What Every Successful Woman Needs to Know to Avoid Being Ripped Off!"* has been empowering investors and business owners since 2010.

Trish is married to Justin. They celebrated twenty years of marriage in 2012. They have three beautiful, rambunctious daughters; Chelsea, and identical twins, Felicity and Olivia.

The Jenkins family lives just north of Brisbane, Australia and are members of Citipointe Church. Trish is a member of Soroptimist International which works for the elevation of women's status around the world. She is also a member of several professional business and women's groups. Trish is an avid networker because "business is all about people!"

KEYNOTE SPEAKING

Trish is available for:

Keynote speaking

Seminars

Workshops

Ministry

Trish speaks in Australia and Internationally.

For more information, please visit:

For Business

www.speakertrishjenkins.com

PH: 61 418 556 198

For Christian Organisations

www.trishjenkinsfaith.com

PH: 61 418 556 198

Weapons of Cash Destruction:
Protect your Fortune from Fraud!

This book is for men.

 It tells you

- ✓ How to spot fraud
- ✓ What makes you a target for financial or romantic fraud
- ✓ What to do about it!

Find it at www.speakertrishjenkins.com

Or go to Amazon and type in the title and author.

DANGEROUS WEALTH: What Every Successful Woman Needs to Know to Avoid Being Ripped Off!

The Good, the Bad and the Ugly: A politically incorrect guide to avoiding or bouncing back from financial and romantic fraud.

Are there really warning signals? YES!

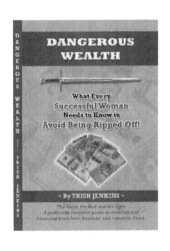

In this book you will discover:

✓ How to recognise warning signals in Business and Romance!

✓ How predators choose their prey!

✓ Types of scams and how to spot them!

✓ Why 'The Secret' can actually attract fraud into your life!

✓ How to turn setbacks into success!

✓ The Warrior Princess within you!

www.speakertrishjenkins.com

Made in the USA
Middletown, DE
03 July 2016